Think Marketing

Think Marketing

by Keith Sparling

The Industrial Society

First published 1989 by
The Industrial Society Press
Robert Hyde House
48 Bryanston Square
London W1H 7LN
01-262-2401

British Library Cataloguing in Publication Data
Sparling, Keith
Think marketing
1. Marketing
I. Title
658.8

ISBN 08529 0455 X

Cover design by Philippa Bramson
Cover illustration by Raymond Carter

Typeset by Ace Filmsetting Limited, Frome, Somerset
Printed in Great Britain by Biddles Limited, Guildford, Surrey

CONTENTS

FOREWORD

In a competitive world, marketing is a crucial element in the success of any organisation. Increasingly companies are finding that the competitive edge is gained through realising the potential of *all* their employees.

No manager can be expected to know everything. But *every* manager should be aware of the basic marketing principles which guide and generate sales for their company's products or services. *Think Marketing* will help all managers—including those with no marketing knowledge—to understand this fundamental concept.

In the end, of course, marketing is all about people. It is an organisation's commitment to quality, service and customer care that are the true hallmarks of excellence. Good marketing is a major step on that journey.

Alistair Graham
Director

INTRODUCTION

Marketing is crucial to the success of any company; without a successful marketing operation the company is doomed. Its products or services may be the best available, but if people are not buying them then the company will die.

There are various approaches to marketing. The one that comes most readily to the mind is the hard sell approach: the company uses aggressive techniques, such as blanket advertising, inertia selling and frequent and deafening repetitions of the injunction to buy, buy, buy. In the short term this can be effective, but the barrage has to be maintained—which is obviously expensive. The turnover of customers is high. People who were initially persuaded to buy the product realise that it is not what they want, and so next time they buy something different. So in order to counter the lack of repeat orders, the company must constantly be seeking new customers. Doing so becomes more difficult as time goes on, not just because the number of potential new customers is steadily shrinking but also because previous customers are telling friends and acquaintances about the competitor products they have discovered. Another factor to consider is that many people assume that, if a company adopts the hard sell, its products must be so poor that there is no other way of marketing them.

If a company is to become successful and remain so it must concentrate much of its efforts on repeat sales. It is not enough to capture new customers: those customers must be retained, so that they use the company's products or services again in the future. For example, an advertisement may induce someone to try a new brand of instant coffee, but there has to be some suitable incentive for the person to continue using that brand in preference to the one he or she bought previously. In the short term after the product's launch, it is possible to create new buying habits using such techniques as special-offer coupons on the label – '10p off the next jar you buy' – but this cannot be carried on indefinitely. Once your brand of instant coffee loses its price advantage (or its perceived price advantage) customers are likely to revert to their previous buying habits. Unless, that is, customers find that they like your coffee better than its competitors.

This is an important point. Just as the best of products has no hope if it is supported by a third-rate marketing operation, so the best of marketing operations is likely to be unsuccessful if the product fails to satisfy the customer. This does not necessarily mean that the product must be *better* than the others on the market. An example can be found in the field of the national newspapers. Nobody could pretend that the best-selling tabloids are in any sense better newspapers than the 'qualities'—in fact, in some cases it is difficult to categorise them as newspapers at all. However, they are successful because their readers derive satisfaction from one issue and therefore buy the next. They are *perceived* by a certain percentage of the population as being better newspapers.

The message of this book, therefore, is concerned with customer-oriented marketing, and in the way in which marketing considerations should be involved at every level and in every aspect of a company's activities. Thomas Alva Edison realised this. He and his workers created the electric lightbulb not as an intellectual exercise but because Edison saw that such a product would have a huge market, and set about devising the product. In other words, the initial concept was a marketing one. Once his company had produced the lightbulb, Edison marketed it effectively, at the same time taking out patents covering every individual aspect of it that he could. The rest, as they say, is history—but there is a part of that history which it is well worth remembering. Around the same time as Edison, Joseph Swan invented the lightbulb, too. However, he was little concerned with marketing it and less active in taking out patents (itself a form of marketing).

Who was the more successful businessman? The answer is obvious: Edison thought first of the customer and of that customer's possible wants, and once he had the required product he devoted his energies to marketing it effectively. The customers were happy—and so, no doubt, was Edison's bank manager.

Another American with a similar marketing consciousness was Walt Disney. He perceived that there was a market for full-length animated movies at a time when everyone else thought that no one would want to watch a 90-minute cartoon, that customers would be bored. Disney's response was that viewers would only be bored if the movie was poorly made. He therefore concentrated on excellence. Fortunately his financial backers agreed with him. Excellence is not cheap: the project exceeded its budgeted costs many times over, and came to be known in Hollywood as 'Disney's Folly'. He then added to his already vast expenses by paying for a brilliant marketing campaign. The result of his efforts was one of the most profitable movies of all time—*Snow White and the Seven Dwarfs*. Like Edison, Disney had started off by thinking of the customer's likely wants, found the best way of satisfying them, and then marketed the product.

If marketing should permeate all of a company's activities, then clearly it is the duty of all managers, whatever their specific areas of responsibility, to have some knowledge of how marketing works. So before you start thinking that merely by reading this book you can turn yourself from an art manager (or whatever) into a marketing manager, it should be emphasised that this is an introductory survey only. To cover the whole area of marketing in depth would require a book many times the size of this one. However, an art manager reading this book should become just a little bit more of a marketing manager—and that is exactly as it should be.

THE MARKETING CONCEPT AND AUDIT

The concept of marketing is not new. All it means is that an organisation should be based on satisfying the needs of the consumer, or end-user, and making a profit by so doing. There are other, more sophisticated, descriptions of the concept. For example, the Institute of Marketing (approved by their National Council: London, 1975) states that:

> Marketing is the management process responsible for identifying, anticipating and satisfying customer requirements profitably.

M. J. Kazimirski in *Creating a Market* (Management Development Branch, International Labour Office: Geneva) has produced this definition:

> Marketing is the performance by an enterprise of all activities required in order to create, promote, and distribute products in accordance with the present or potential customers' demand and the firm's ability to produce.

And William J. Stanton, Professor of Marketing at the University of Colorado, in *Fundamentals of Marketing* (Maidenhead: McGraw Hill, 1967) defines marketing as:

> a total system of interacting business activities designed to plan, price, promote and distribute want-satisfying products and services to present and potential customers.

These definitions have important implications. Marketing

is shown as recognising the *needs and wants of customers*. The definitions suggest that marketing is a total, integrated process rather than a fragmented assortment of functions. Marketing is, in fact, the result of the interaction of these and other activities. The term 'selling' is often used erroneously as a synonym for 'marketing', but selling is merely one method of promotion, and promotion itself is only a part of the marketing programme. Theodore Levitt in an article in *The Harvard Business Review* entitled 'Marketing Myopia', has spelled out the difference between selling and marketing:

> Selling focuses on the needs of the seller, marketing on the needs of the buyer. Selling is pre-occupied with the seller's need to convert his product into cash; marketing with the idea of satisfying the needs of the customer by means of the product and a whole cluster of things associated with creating, delivering and finally consuming it.

It is vital that everyone involved in business should accept and understand the idea that industry is a consumer-satisfying process and *not* simply a goods-producing process.

The principal marketing functions

A marketing function may be defined as a group of activities involved in the marketing of goods or services. According to the modern marketing concept there are four major functions:

- marketing information
- product planning
- selling and distribution
- advertising and promotion

Marketing information

Marketing is based on customers, and so the starting point for marketing is to learn about those customers: who they are, where they are, what they want and why they buy. If you do not know enough about your potential customers, you will waste money and time on developing the wrong products, on misdirected promotion, on inappropriate methods of distribution, and so forth.

It is one thing to know a lot about a few customers. It is something else to know a lot about the market as a whole. Marketing research is the tool we employ to learn about customers. All companies use it to some degree—some without even realising it. Talks with customers, feedback from representatives, keeping up to date with trade or professional journals—all of these are forms of marketing research. But the information gained in these ways can give a much clearer picture if it is collected methodically and backed up by properly collated statistics.

Marketing research need not be elaborate, but it must be objective and systematic. Useful information is a matter of quality rather than of quantity—of asking the right questions and then interpreting the answers intelligently.

Product planning

Customers do not buy 'products' as such, but rather what it is that the products will do for them. For example, consumers do not buy washing machines—they buy the capability to do the wash more quickly and more easily.

New products and/or services are essential to the survival and growth of all companies, but in today's competitive conditions the risks entailed in developing them are formidable. Marketing research provides the necessary knowledge about the market and about the needs and desires of the users. Product planning converts this knowledge into acceptable and saleable products (taking into consideration technical capabilities). Like each of the other marketing functions, product planning is a continuing process. It goes on throughout a product's life, from conception to the 'commercialisation' stage, right through until the product is finally withdrawn from the market.

In practice, all products and services are a compromise between what customers need and what it is possible to produce at a reasonable cost. The skill in product planning can therefore be seen to lie in converting an organisation's inherited or acquired skills and facilities into products and services which yield customer value and satisfaction while at the same time making a profit.

The evolution of a product within an organisation must be a group effort, in which the physical technicalities of production can be matched with the requirements of the marketing operation. The starting point, however, is an assessment of the market: the forces at work, the factors which motivate the customers, and the personality or image required of the product.

Selling and distribution

Knowing about the market and then providing appropriate products is not enough. Sooner or later somebody else will do the same thing, and more conveniently for your customers. Your organisation must provide channels so that products can be distributed from where they are made to where customers want to find them. Distribution can be direct, through wholesalers, or through retailers—or through a combination of all three. The decision as to which course you adopt depends upon marketing information.

Apart from determining the channels of distribution, marketing has an interest in seeing that the methods of distribution - secondary distribution points, delivery, and so on - meet customer requirements at the lowest reasonable cost. Customers at all levels – wholesale, retail, consumer or end-user – are personally interested in the way goods are distributed to them. They appreciate good stocks, convenient warehousing and prompt, courteous and reliable service.

Of course, providing suitable products and having a good system of distribution will not automatically ensure customer demand if the customers are not even aware of your product's existence. The sales function is a major tactic in the presentation of the product to the customer.

The importance of selling and distribution is in no way diminished when management adopts a marketing perspective. In actual fact, the marketing concept enhances the status and role of selling by placing greater emphasis on marketing requirements than on production needs. Also, selling, as a part of marketing, becomes more effective because of the closer integration with advertising and sales promotion, product planning and marketing research. Another point is that the marketing perspective involves a fundamental shift in emphasis away from the needs and convenience of the *manufacturer* or *distributor* towards the needs and convenience of the *buyer*. This means that the company's sales force and distribution methods must be tailored to the requirements of the customers and concentrate on ways of helping those customers with their problems.

Advertising and sales promotion

The fourth major marketing function concerns:

- advertising to the customer or user in all media (TV, press, radio, trade journals, and so on)
- consumer and trade sales promotion
- public and press mentions

The purpose of each and every advertisement, no matter what the medium being used, is to influence certain people to think or act in a certain way favourable to the advertiser. The basic task of advertising is to convey a message of one sort or another to a target audience. The members of that audience might be the general public, general trade buyers, specifiers or purchasing officers or other special groups of people. The message has the primary aim of changing or reinforcing people's attitude of mind. Its secondary aim is to influence their behaviour.

Sales promotion is the vital link between personal selling by the sales representative and the advertising directed towards consumers and trade customers. It uses various techniques in an endeavour to provide special incentives to buy.

Three basic groups of activities are involved. First are specific incentives provided by producers of consumer goods in an attempt to persuade the consumer to buy particular products at particular times. Such tactics are described as 'consumer promotions', and might include free samples, banded pack offers, couponing, competitions and the like. The second activity, 'trade promotions', is aimed at distributors and wholesalers, hoping to persuade them actively to sell the products and to put that little bit of extra effort behind the products. To this end, the manufacturer may use special cash discounts, bonuses, sales competitions, and so forth. The third group of activities can be generally described as 'display'. Under this heading come product display, window banners, dump-bins, shelf-talkers, etc.

Public relations has been defined by the Institute of Public Relations as 'the *deliberate, planned* and *sustained* effort to establish and maintain a mutual understanding between an organisation and its publics'. The sales-promotion activities described above are concerned with making a sale that was instigated by the creation, through media advertising, of a desire to purchase. If the organisation's marketing approach is sufficiently well balanced, the sale will be a source of satisfaction to both buyer and seller. A favourable two-way regard will have been built up by good public and press relations. Public relations covers many activities—company livery, product presentation, telephone or reception manners, and a host of others. Press relations is a part of public relations in that it endeavours to achieve good editorial coverage for the organisation in all the relevant media.

Preparing a marketing plan

One of the simplest and yet probably the most neglected means of increasing marketing effectiveness is to ensure that all marketing activities subscribe to a common objective. In other words, an organisation should have an overall marketing plan.

Marketing planning is not new. It has been practised since the beginning of business history. The first Phoenician to have the idea of sailing from home to trade with the peoples of other nations was planning his marketing activities.

Like a philosophy or a personality, a marketing plan is something which a business *has*, even if no one in the organisation has any idea of what a marketing plan actually is. A marketing plan may be effective or ineffective, stable or changing, but the simple fact is that it is there.

In thinking of marketing planning, it is of prime importance to recognise that the plan has to be market-oriented rather than product-oriented. In other words, the plan must be directed to meeting the needs of a particular market rather than just selling a product.

A product often has several distinct markets, and separate sub-plans must be made for each market. For example, a maker of motor accessories would need one plan for selling electrical fittings as original equipment to car manufacturers and an entirely different plan for selling the fittings through garage outlets as spare parts.

Defining the target market

Since the plan is to be *market*-oriented, it is necessary to define the target market. If this is defined too broadly – 'the market for automotive accessories', for example – the plan will fail to pinpoint specific opportunities and activities. Perhaps the most practical criteria to consider when separating markets are, first, end-use of the product and, second, the channel of distribution.

The recognition of a separate market – one which has previously been dealt with only as part of a larger one, if at all – can sometimes trigger a major breakthrough. For example, a few years ago a major home-appliance manufacturer recognised the home-building market as being separate from that involving the retail sales of appliances. The manufacturer reaped the benefits of increased sales before its competitors realised that this distinct market existed. To take another example, a publishing company produced one of the first books on holography for the lay reader. The book sold respectably in bookshops. However, one of the company's representatives realised that there was another market – people interested in holograms rather than people interested in books. He generated a whole string of new customers for the publisher – and his commission soared.

An essential survival factor for many companies, particularly the smaller ones, is their ability to identify relatively unknown or hidden markets and to target them—that is, to develop marketing plans tailored to the unique requirements of those markets.

The written plan

The essence of effective marketing is to work out a sound and reasoned plan. But marketing plans are vulnerable things. Advertising people and sales people have a great sense of moment and their sudden inspirations – their 'good ideas at the time' – can drastically affect the marketing plan, often for the worse. How can one prevent this?

The answer is: *write it down*. Written plans have to be developed so that the entire organisation can be appraised of the company's position in the market, or in each separate target market, and all personnel concerned can contribute to the planning involved so that the desired objectives can be achieved.

The main reasons why formal marketing plans are often not prepared are the belief that a written plan precludes flexibility, the fact that time is at a premium, and the mistaken belief that a written plan is simply not necessary. However, like it or lump it, a written plan is the only foolproof way of holding together the host of sub-plans – product development, field selling and distribution, merchandising plans, and so on – which taken all together make up the overall strategic plan. The document is vital, too, in its role of setting out explicitly and in detail who is responsible for accomplishing each element. Executives working in different marketing areas – advertising, production, and so on – can see their own roles in relation to the marketing effort as a whole.

The elements of the marketing plan

The cost of planning is insignificant in comparison with the funds that may be spent on advertising and promotion. And it is well to remember that, even if you have the best sales force, the best creative staff and the best media programme in the world, you will not be able to match those of your competitors who have superior marketing ideas and programmes.

The actual format of a marketing plan will vary according to the needs of each company. However, if it is to be complete, a marketing plan should have the following elements:

- *Situation analysis*—this is an objective analysis of the company's position in relation to the market and the competition at the time the plan is drawn up. It is diagnostic. Its aim is to determine 'exactly where are we?' in detail.
- *Statement of marketing goals and objectives*—having established where you are in relation to the market and your customers, it is reasonable to ask: 'Where do we want to go?'
- *The marketing sub-plans*—the plan commences with a 'strategy statement' which is to be the basis for a detailed plan of action. The strategy should answer the question: 'How are we going to do it?'

Let us look at these components of the marketing plan a little more closely.

Situation analysis

This section enumerates all the major facts about the market, the consumer, the competition, industrial practices and the company product or products. It looks at the size and scope of the market and the organisation's share of it; the sales, costs and gross profit histories of the products; distribution channels (buying habits and attitudes, selling practices, trade advertising, point-of-sale display material *vs* competition, etc.); the consumer or end-user (attitudes, purchasing and usage habits, the advertising history of the product, etc.); the product itself (history of product development, packaging, pricing, comparison with competition, etc.).

Before the setting out of the marketing goals and objectives, the close of the situation analysis can very usefully contain a section headed something like 'Problems and Opportunities'. The 'facts' developed in the situation analysis constitute the basis for this section. Here the most important findings are summarised and pinpointed, either as problems which need to be overcome or opportunities on which the company may capitalise.

Statement of marketing goals and objectives

In this section is detailed as far as possible what you wish to attain in respect of market penetration, profits, product range and so on over the next year, two years, five years, or whatever. Objectives should be clear, definitive statements of what is intended to happen and when. The key to writing objectives is to make them specific.

Use the company goal to establish the overall outline of where you want to be at the end of a specific time period. The objectives should be analysed into a series of subject areas:

- sales volume
- market share
- distribution
- packaging
- pricing/profits
- manufacturing/production
- product range
- advertising
- sales promotion
- public relations
- customer servicing
- merchandising
- market research
- competition

The marketing sub-plans

This section of the overall plan is subdivided into two parts: long-term (strategical) and short-term (tactical) aims.

The 'strategy' subsection covers, in a broad fashion, long-range plans concerning sales volume, pricing, media, product development, and so on. Clearly ideas, imagination and creativity are required when drawing up this subsection. However, since the objectives have already been established in the previous section, it is now possible to weigh up each idea against the relevant objectives and select the one which can best be developed to meet those objectives. The specific long-range marketing methods by which you hope to reach the objectives should be worked out using the same list of marketing areas as you used in the previous section of the plan when discussing the objectives themselves.

The period covered by the 'strategy' subsection will probably be in the range of two to five years. The 'tactics' subsection of the plan should cover only the first year. Here are itemised who does what, with whom, when and where, and the costs involved. Immediate and specific advertising and promotional considerations are dealt with. Also in this subsection you should discuss the specific plans or programmes for the twelve-month period. The marketing areas covered are the same as before, but now you are looking at them in detail rather than merely considering them broadly.

Using the marketing plan

To prevent the marketing plan from becoming a sort of archival document, doing nothing more useful than gather dust on departmental shelves, you must treat it as an 'action' document. A complete copy should be given to every member of the company responsible for carrying out any function described in it. A single person should be nominated to be responsible for seeing that it is carried out as written, or to give approval to any and all deviations.

The plan should be reviewed regularly to check progress against the previously agreed goals. In addition, a monthly report on progress is useful and effective. Although the plan may have been written to cover a period of up to ten years, it must remain flexible. Basic changes in the product or market will require the rewriting of sub-plans. Even in the unlikely event of there being no changes over a twelve-month period, the marketing plan should be completely reviewed and re-evaluated at least once a year.

Summarising, a marketing plan can be defined as a written document which:

- examines the major facts in the marketing situation under consideration
- identifies the problems and opportunities inherent in the particular marketing situation
- establishes specific long- and short-range marketing objectives for the product
- proposes a long-range strategy to solve the problems and to capitalise on the opportunities
- recommends specific product-development, selling, advertising and promotional tactics to carry out short-range aims and accomplish the objectives set for the next twelve-month period

The marketing audit

A marketing audit can be defined as:

> A systematic, critical, and unbiased review and appraisal of the basic objectives and policies of the marketing function and of the organisation, methods, procedures, and personnel employed to implement the policies and achieve the objectives.

Although the word 'audit' suggests that this is an after-the-fact review of a marketing operation, the marketing audit includes an evaluation of the effects of hypothetical alternatives before it comes to any conclusion. Thus the audit becomes a very important tool in helping you to decide future strategy and tactics. In addition to identifying weaknesses in the marketing operation and programme, it recommends ways and means of capitalising on strong points.

A marketing audit provides two main checks: first, that the company is headed in a profitable direction and, second, that all its marketing activities are geared to using its resources effectively.

Considerable stress needs to be laid on the independent, objective character that the audit should have and on the total freedom of inquiry allowed to the person who carries it out. Only if these conditions are met can a marketing audit fulfil its triple purpose of determining just what is being done, appraising and evaluating the achievements, and formulating recommendations for future policy and practice.

A company that is not sure why it is in business and is attached to a declining market could perhaps be saved from extinction by a timely marketing audit. At the other end of the scale, a company heading in a profitable direction with clear objectives, appropriate policies and well chosen products and markets might think that there was little need to conduct a marketing audit. However, marketing audits are as important for successful organisations as for any other. Factors that have made a company successful are, at times, the ones that can bring about its downfall. For example, the company's success may be the result of dynamic policies and methods which were decided years ago but have little relevance to today's environment.

A marketing audit, then, is concerned not only with the way things are and should be done now: it is vitally concerned also with the orderly and balanced development of marketing activities in the years to come. Too often marketing audits are used only when a company gets into difficulties. This is to take a ridiculously narrow view of their purpose and potential. Once it is accepted that marketing audits can benefit successful as well as troubled companies, it follows that they should be scheduled fairly regularly.

A distinction can be drawn between the system-level (horizontal) and the activity-level (vertical) marketing audit. Both levels cover the same ground – objectives, programme, implementation, and organisation – but in different ways.

The horizontal audit is an attempt to develop a total evaluation of the company's marketing effort. It examines all the elements that go into the marketing whole, with particular emphasis upon the relationships of these elements to each other within the marketing 'mix'. The vertical audit usually comes after the horizontal audit, which has identified those marketing activities that need closer examination. The vertical audit singles out these elements and subjects them to thorough study and examination.

A company can have a marketing audit performed in a variety of ways. The paramount considerations are the auditor's objectivity, analytical mind and knowledge of marketing practice. Other considerations include the cost involved and how seriously the company needs a good audit.

Because of the wide range that has to be covered and the depth to which the individual activities must be studied, a marketing audit should not be hurried. Equally important, though, is the fact that if the audit drags on too long the information may be out of date by the time the recommendations are ready. Accordingly, a sensible timetable needs to be drawn up beforehand and, barring unforeseen circumstances, adhered to.

The horizontal marketing audit

The first step in a horizontal marketing audit is to obtain a clear statement of the company's marketing objectives. This is often quite a difficult task. Next the auditor must appraise how well (or how badly) those objectives tap the company's resources. It is sometimes hard to draw a sharp dividing line between objectives and policies. The auditor has to differentiate between the goals (the objectives) set by the company and the way in which those targets are to be achieved (the policies).

In these early stages the auditor's concern is to determine whether or not the objectives are sufficiently marketing-oriented. He or she can make an important contribution to the company's welfare by impressing upon management the desirability (under most circumstances) of reorienting marketing objectives so that they relate to customers' needs rather than company products, and to creating customer satisfaction rather than just sales volume.

The next stage concerns the company's policies. The auditor's task is to evaluate how efficiently the present company programme is structured. He or she will want to examine how the marketing budget is allocated to various elements of the marketing 'mix' and to the various target markets. An objective appraisal of the balance of the company's marketing activities is one of the prime responsibilities of this part of the audit.

The auditor is concerned also with organisation and personnel. The appraisal here focuses on two related things: first, an evaluation of authority and power related to lines of authority and responsibility; second, the adequacy of the personnel both as a group and in terms of those individuals occupying key jobs. This stage of the audit often highlights such common weaknesses as lack of job specification, 'missing' responsibilities, various activities being out of phase, and people reporting to more than one manager.

The final stage of the horizontal marketing audit analyses the company's existing procedures. It asks who does what, when and how. In some companies, procedures are formally estabished and recognised; in others, procedures are completely informal. The auditor seeks to examine the more important procedures to see whether they could be improved.

The vertical marketing audit

Following a horizontal audit, it is likely that some particular activities will seem to cry out for a more detailed appraisal.

The framework outlined above in terms of the horizontal audit is used also for the auditing of any specific marketing activity. For example, it might be felt necessary to carry out a distribution audit—appraising various distribution channels, studying the level of penetration into retail outlets, and so forth. The auditor concentrates on the same four factors as for the horizontal audit: objectives, policies, organisation and personnel, and finally procedures. In other words, he or she is trying to answer the following questions:

- What are you trying to do?
- How are you going about it?
- Have you got the right people in the right places, and is the organisation such that they can do their jobs as well as they might?
- Are the established procedures in your company as good as they could be?

Undertaking the marketing audit

Choosing who should perform the audit is a delicate matter. The final selection, and the decision as to how many people should be involved, depend on the company's size and resources. There is no hard-and-fast rule. Three ways of carrying out marketing audits may be considered:

- *Having the line managers carry out the audit.* This may seem inexpensive, but there are several drawbacks. Usually line managers lack the necessary time to carry out a full-fledged audit and are anyway not in a position to assess marketing operations objectively. It is possible, too, that they will be reluctant to criticise any of their own earlier decisions.

- *Setting up an audit department.* This can be a very good way of training marketing executives and giving them a chance to introduce change. Again, however, it is difficult for inside auditors, no matter how conscientious they may be, to remain unbiased.
- *Commissioning an independent marketing consultant.* There are three basic advantages here. First, the consultant has broad experience in many different kinds of companies and many different industries. Second, the required objectivity is the stock-in-trade of the qualified consultant. Third, the consultant can give the necessary time and concentrated effort so that the marketing audit can be comprehensive.

Implications of the marketing audit

To summarise, the marketing auditor seeks to discover whether or not the company's objectives are clear, specific and market-oriented. With respect to policies, he or she seeks to evaluate company decisions on the allocation and mix of current marketing efforts. Third, the auditor seeks to evaluate the adequacy of the company's organisation and the effectiveness of its personnel. Finally, he or she appraises the procedures used in the marketing operation.

Most company executives would claim – quite rightly – that they were constantly evaluating their operations. But the marketing audit, in its capacity to stand slightly 'aside', does more than this. In covering the marketing process itself, what the company is aiming at, the way it is going about it, and what it has available to carry out the function, the audit plays a fundamental role in the vital process of keeping a company's marketing policies and practices in constant adjustment with the market.

MARKETING MANAGEMENT

Marketing management involves integrating all those activities of a company that contribute to marketing. This is done under the direction of a top executive, the marketing manager, who bears overall responsibility for:

- analysing markets
- creating new products and packaging
- pricing
- physical distribution
- selling
- distribution channels
- budgeting
- advertising and promotion
- customer and distribution-channel relations
- coordination of manufacturing, finance and marketing

The basic functions of the marketing manager are to plan and manage all aspects of the marketing programme, to maintain and equip a well trained organisation to carry out the marketing programme, and to direct all marketing operations in such a way as to attain the stated objectives within the constraints of company policy, budgets and required levels of profitability. In order to achieve all of this, the marketing manager has various responsibilities, either directly or through managers reporting back:

- sales planning, control and policy
- sales organisation
- market forecasting
- setting and achieving sales targets
- public relations
- product development and planning
- consumer research, product research, market research, sales research, motivational research
- employee relations within his or her department

The marketing manager must be involved at the beginning of any product-planning cycle, rather than just in the final stages. As he or she deals with product development from the inception of the idea right through to the point of purchase, the marketing manager will have to work closely with other members of the company. These people will all have to be directed towards a common objective, the successful marketing of the product. Their various contributions will be in the areas of:

- finance
- purchasing
- research and development
- marketing research
- production
- advertising
- sales and (probably) servicing personnel at different management levels

The market research expert, the sales manager, the accountant—all of these people have quite different world-views. The sales manager, for example, will generally be more conscious of sales volume than of profitability, and may well feel that his or her work is constantly hampered by accountants, production people and research experts, who seem unwilling to allow the production of the range of goods which the sales manager would like to sell. Similarly, the advertising manager (or agency) may feel that increased sales depend upon advertising alone, and have little notion of the part played by all the other departments. The marketing manager needs the co-operation and support of these and all the other middle-management personnel. He or she must weld together their talents and experience and decide on the plan of action which is in the best interests of the company.

We shall discuss the efforts of the marketing manager under four broad headings:

- marketing activities
- principles of marketing management
- marketing techniques
- marketing strategy

Marketing activities

There are eight basic marketing activities:

1 *Marketing research*. Broadly this means all the activities concerned with obtaining market and marketing information. Such information is necessary so that decisions can be based on facts rather than guesswork.
2 *Product planning*. This is concerned with developing a product and its packaging. Its aim is to satisfy the potential consumer (or end-user) and enable the company to use its production facilities to the full.
3 *Pricing*. This activity is concerned with determining the price of the product. There are a number of considerations: production costs must be weighed against market factors such as distribution, discounts, competitive price levels and what the consumer is likely to be prepared to pay.
4 *Sales management*, which is concerned with administration of the selling programme and the selection of the most effective and economical methods of selling, either to retail-

ers or directly to the customers. Sales management is concerned also with grading, training, motivation and control of the sales force.

5 *Advertising*. This leads the customer to the product by making it known and creating a demand.

6 *Sales promotion*. Sales promotion pushes the product towards the user. Basically, this term covers all activities relating to sales and selling other than advertising.

7 *Public relations*. This is directly concerned with that part of the marketing 'mix' which affects the company's relationships with its markets (or publics).

8 *Distribution*, which is concerned with getting the product from the manufacturer to the customer at wholesale, retail and/or consumer (end-user) levels.

Principles of marketing management

The first principle is that the company must have an *active attitude* towards the market. It cannot expect consumers to buy a product simply because it has been produced. A company with the right attitude will study the market, promote the product, persuade the customers and make the product available and easy to buy. The second principle is that the company must accept that marketing should be recognised as having at least as much importance as the other management functions—production, finance and administration.

The third principle is that marketing must be 'integrated'. In effect, this means that marketing considerations - customer preferences, competitive activity, and so on - must be taken into account not just by the marketing department but by production, finance and administrative personnel at management level. It is part of the job of the marketing manager to provide the production personnel with clear definitions of what the consumers most desire in a given product, what price they will pay for it, where and when it will be bought, why people will want to buy it, and so on. Other departments must similarly be kept in touch.

An overriding principle is that, throughout all the stages of product planning, production scheduling, determining channels of distribution, sales strategy and product stock levels, and finally coping with physical distribution, the requirements of the consumer should be taken into account.

Marketing techniques

Modern social sciences - economics, statistics and applied psychology - all play a part in the technique of marketing. Marketing skills and techniques can be divided into four main groups.

First there is marketing information. In many marketing activities, management wants to obtain certain data—who will buy the product, when, where and how they will buy it, etc. If the marketing manager can answer these questions correctly, he or she is on the way towards securing a footing in the marketplace. This information, and much more besides, is available through research—consumer, product sales operations, communications and economic and business research. Each of these topics is discussed more fully in the next chapter.

The second group of marketing techniques consists of those intended to influence the consumer and stimulate demand for the product—advertising, sales promotion and the gaining of mentions in the media.

A third group of skills involves the analysis of data. The marketing manager needs to have a logical approach to problem analysis and solving—whether the problem concerned is a difficult one, such as the decision to drop a middleman in a particular distribution channel, or a comparatively simple one, such as how to raise the call/sales ratio of a particular sales representative.

The fourth and final group of techniques can be broadly defined as practical marketing skills. These skills are applied by specialists in particular marketing activities. Market researchers, public-relations consultants, packaging consultants, sales trainers, work-study engineers, advertising agencies and many other specialists are available to the marketing manager.

Marketing strategy

The characteristics of the seller, the product and the market all serve as constraints on your choice of marketing strategy. The most important factors to take into account when selecting a strategy are: company resources, product variables or differentials, the stage the product has reached in its life cycle, the type of market and its degree of segmentation, and the marketing strategies used by your competitors.

The growth of a company can be implemented through four basic product/market strategies:

1 *Market penetration.* The company seeks to increase sales for its existing products in its existing markets through more aggressive promotion and distribution.
2 *Market development.* The company seeks increased sales by taking its existing products into new markets.
3 *Product development.* The company seeks to increase sales by developing improved products for its existing markets.
4 *Diversification.* The company seeks increased sales by developing new products for new markets.

Marketing organisation

Before we study in detail the various types of marketing organisations, we shall look at the transitional stages through which a company passes as it goes from being a production-oriented organisation to a marketing-oriented one.

Company organisation in which marketing activities are fragmented

The main characteristic of this sort of company is the absence of coordination between sales, market information, advertising, production planning and budgeting. Each of these activities is recognised, and has been made the responsibility of one or other of the middle-management team, but they are not grouped according to any functional rationale. Neither are they under the control of one coordinating executive. Market forecasting is regarded as nothing more than a financial exercise. Marketing research is unlikely to be understood, let alone be made actionable by the production manager. And warehousing is not seen as one of the responsibilities of the sales manager.

Company organisation where sales management is beginning to be viewed more broadly

In this sort of company there is evident a noticeable increase in the responsibilities of the sales manager. Certain activities previously undertaken by other members of middle management have been regrouped and are now controlled and coordinated by the sales manager. However, not all of the key marketing responsibilities have been brought together under a single management executive. The responsibility for distribution rests with the distribution manager, production scheduling is the sole prerogative of the production manager, and so on.

Company organisation embracing the concept of marketing management

The transition to a fully fledged marketing organisation is often gradual. There are several ways in which a company can evolve towards the marketing concept:

- Centralising head office. Locating all management personnel in the same office encourages managers of different divisions to get together and work out coordinated marketing programmes.
- Consolidating field-sales offices. The consolidation of field-sales offices encourages joint campaigns, the sharing of specialised personnel and wider range setting. Customers receive a better service, and unnecessary duplication of marketing effort is reduced.
- Centralising marketing staffs. Arranging that the key marketing functions (advertising, marketing research, and so on) are carried out on a centralised basis, rather than at the divisional level, encourages a coordinated, total-company marketing approach.
- Specialising sales groups. Specialised sales groups can be set up to sell the products of several different divisions to particular market segments. The market segments concerned can be defined in terms of the end-users, the distribution channels, the intermediate distributors (e.g., agents), or simply geography.
- Selling to key accounts. As their customers' business operations increase in scope, companies often set up key-accounts sales managers. These executives can represent all divisions of the company or just a selection, but their marketing efforts are oriented towards individual key accounts.

Types of marketing organisation

Probably the most common organisation within a marketing-oriented company is that in which the chief marketing executive works through managers who each have a special function. Under this arrangement, the basic organisational unit is the marketing function—sales, product planning, advertising, etc. For example, the head of sales reports to the marketing manager and is responsible for handling field selling and sales administration. A separate marketing services unit reports to the marketing manager and handles marketing research, product/market planning, advertising, sales promotion, sales budgeting, forecasting and distribution.

This form of organisation – which has the prime advantage of simplicity – may be found useful when:

- relatively few products are sold in relatively few markets
- specialisation by function is considered desirable
- it is wished to centralise authority and responsibility in a single marketing executive

As the business grows, products and markets become more diverse. This tends to cause strains on a purely functional organisation. For example, problems may arise with regard to proper allocations of selling time, advertising appropriations, and so forth. It may therefore become opportune to consider one or several of the more sophisticated types of organisation.

The advantages of product specialisation become apparent when a company's range of products becomes so extensive that a simple functional arrangement is no longer effective. To be certain that each product receives the attention and support it deserves, management may consider some form of product-line orientation within the marketing organisation. Although there are many variations of this type of organisation, there are four basic patterns: product divisions, market groups, product sales forces and product managers.

Product divisions

Under this plan, the company is divisionalised: a separate self-sustaining unit is organised for each major product or product group. This is usually the preferred organisational approach when each product group really represents a different business which is large enough – or potentially large enough – to support its own production and marketing operations.

Market groups

Where customers fall into distinctly different market groups in terms of buying patterns or product interest, the marketing organisation may be best centred on market managers. In most of the cases where this makes organisational sense, the company is highly technical in its activity, often having a very narrow product range. The sales force is usually highly specialised and requires technical back-up.

Within this structure, market managers report to the senior executive. In turn, each market (or customer) manager supervises functional managers who deal with sales, marketing services, etc. The major advantage of market specialisation is that it leads to greater expertise and effectiveness in marketing to distinct customers or markets.

Product sales forces

Instead of separate divisions or marketing groups, the differentiation involved in the product-sales-force plan focuses on the sales operations relevant to each product group. The other marketing functions are performed for all product lines, across the board, by functional specialists. As with the two preceding structures, manufacturing, research and finance remain centralised.

This is the more logical approach when each product is too small for divisionalisation, or when the only area in which product specialisation is important and practical is the sales area. However, such sales structures are often cumbersome, and the development of several sales forces within the company does not make for the most economic use of manpower.

Product managers

In multi-product companies, particularly those in fast-moving consumer goods (fmcg) markets, the product or brand management structure is more evident. The fact that there are different markets and a large number of products with differing profitability curves means that 'competition' is much more a question of brand *versus* brand than company *versus* company. Company profitability is regarded in terms of its being the sum of the individual profitabilities of products or groups of products. Companies which have adopted this concept look upon their product managers as individuals responsible for giving their undivided attention to the business welfare of particular products or groups of products. That is the basic principle; however, the number of ways in which it is brought into practice in different companies is almost limitless. Likewise, between different companies there is also a considerable variation in the nature and scope of the responsibilities assigned to product managers. It is therefore difficult to define precisely the role of the product manager.

Despite the growing acceptance of the concept as a whole, the product manager himself or herself still remains a somewhat controversial figure. At the heart of the debate lies the disagreement concerning the degree of authority and responsibility the product manager should possess and exercise. In terms of the relationship with the rest of the organisation, the product manager is neither a line executive (in that there is no line of authority) and nor is he or she 'staff' in the sense of support staff (as are, for example, market-research or advertising managers). The product manager does not have the unqualified responsibility for seeing that everything related to the product gets done well and on time. The manager's task is to serve as a focal point for the planning and coordination of all the activities required for growth and profitability of the relevant product, and it is in this *planning* role that the responsibilities of the job lie.

Organisation planning factors

The organisational implications of the total marketing concept are clear. Most companies who have adopted the concept have realised the wisdom of having an integrated organisational approach so that a strong, unified marketing effort can be achieved. Instead of allowing sales, advertising and other marketing functions to go their own separate and independent ways, these companies have appointed people to be responsible for coordinating and integrating their efforts in accordance with predetermined objectives, policies and plans, thereby making certain that all marketing activities are conducted with the customer viewpoint uppermost in mind. In large divisionalised companies, this basic responsibility is exercised by the marketing director, and it may also be implemented at lower levels by marketing managers, product managers and people with other titles but similar duties. In smaller companies, the marketing manager takes on the responsibility of integrating the various marketing functions.

In terms of the total marketing concept, *all* functions in the business – not just marketing – look to the marketplace for guidance. Thus marketing, being the function closest to the marketplace, must be organised in relation to the other major functions in such a way that it can provide the necessary leadership and direction.

All marketing organisations, regardless of whether sales and marketing are run separately or together, must be aware of five factors affecting the company:

1 *Company functions*. Sales, advertising, merchandising, distribution, research.
2 *Company products*. Product development and planning.
3 *Geography*—whether centralised or not.
4 *Distributive trade groups*. Direct, wholesale, retail.
5 *Markets*. Specific customers and end-users.

A structure which attempted to place equal emphasis on all these factors would obviously be hopelessly inadequate, both economically and administratively. Choices must be made. All organisational structures have to rely on compromises based on whichever factor is predominantly important.

Planning a marketing structure depends upon careful analysis and evaluation of a large number of external and internal factors. The external factors are those which lie outside the company itself but exert a strong influence on the nature of the marketing organisation. They fall into three main categories:

1 *Business environment*. The type of environment the firm must operate within influences not only its marketing objectives and strategy but also its organisation for implementing them. One environmental influence is the rate of change in the industries being served. If it is high there will have to be more frequent responsive changes in marketing organisation than if it is relatively low. Other environmental variables that must be evaluated include the competitive structure and the nature and length of channels of distribution.
2 *The market - its size, scope, nature and location*. The nature of a company's markets has a strong influence on the type of marketing organisation. When there are relatively few markets, a market-oriented structure is made easier; when a large number of market groups is involved, a product-oriented organisation is more flexible. Markets covering a wide expanse of territory often require some form of geographical organisation unnecessary for more compact markets. The number of customers, their frequency of pur-

chase, size of order, degree of service required and other characteristics are further factors influencing the ultimate form of the marketing organisation.

3 *Customer requirements*. The requirements and expectations of the customer may also have an effect on the marketing organisation. Central buying by giant wholesalers, retail chains and buying syndicates, not to mention the contract procedures upon which they may insist, can be an important factor in this respect.

Then there are the internal factors. As with the external factors, these can be grouped under three main headings:

1 *Management philosophy*. Whether good or bad, implicit or explicit, top management's attitudes and judgements have an important bearing on organisational planning. For example, if management has traditionally held a tight rein on decision making, it is hard to institute a decentralised organisation.

2 *Product policy*. The breadth of the product line often influences the nature of the marketing organisation. As product offerings become increasingly diverse there is a real tendency to move away from a straight functional approach towards a product-group approach, or towards some combination of the two. If company policy dictates that there should be an increasing emphasis on new products and entry into new markets, a market-oriented organisational structure may be in order.

3 *Personnel*. The human beings who are expected to carry out the various functions are an important factor in organisation planning. Human values are critical. Proper decisions cannot be made without due regard to the people involved—their type, number, qualifications, capabilities, responsibilities, personalities, attitudes, ambitions and all sorts of other intangible but important characteristics. Any organisation must to a degree be tailored to the people who will have to make it work. That said, one should not necessarily sacrifice the optimum organisational approach merely

because of the limitations of the people who will be involved in it.

Marketing orientation calls for the use of specialist functions, but at the same time it requires a closer coordination of activities further down the management scale. The increase in the number of functional or specialist activities must not be allowed to generate increases in management levels. Indeed, the opposite is the case. In seeking to coordinate activities the aim should be to *reduce* levels of management as far as possible, bringing together managers of similar or complementary marketing areas so that there is a gradual convergence towards the single objective: profitability.

Industrial and consumer goods

The marketing of industrial goods can involve more complex and widely differing marketing patterns than is the case with most consumer goods, the marketing of which tends to follow a common pattern. These marketing differences are fairly clear, but not always appreciated.

Industrial goods are destined to be used by producers of other goods and services. The customers include firms, factories, mines, farms, contractors and other service industries, institutions and government agencies. Consumer goods, by contrast, are normally for personal or household use and will not receive any further processing. By comparison with most consumer goods and services, the demand for industrial goods can be intermittent and subject to abrupt changes.

Channels of distribution for industrial goods tend to be shorter than those for consumer goods. Industrial-goods suppliers and purchasers are very often in direct contact; alternatively, they may use a few highly specialised middlemen. A biscuit manufacturer might have to sell direct and/or through wholesalers to something like 10,000 retailers before the final consumers can buy the product; the manufacturer has three tasks—to persuade the trade to stock the product, to persuade the consumer to try it, and to keep on reminding people about it so that they will keep on buying it. The manufacturer of industrial goods, by contrast, may have only a few customers, although each of these will have far greater purchasing power. For many industrial-goods manufacturers the total number of buyers is determinable: a small number of major buyers may account for the bulk of a company's output.

The criteria for purchasing industrial goods are primarily technical in nature—efficiency of performance, economy, durability, effects on productivity, and profitability. The customer is normally the user and an expert purchaser; the purchase itself is usually subject to multiple influences, both technical and commercial, within the customer's organisation, and is normally subject to lengthy negotiation. Many industrial goods are supplied on a tendering basis, which raises special problems of estimating and pricing.

Generally speaking, the industrial-goods sales representative is primarily concerned with finding the right people to influence – specifiers, contractors, technical experts, commercial buyers, and so on – thereby paving the way for his or her company's technical experts, who will actually consummate the deal. The consumer-goods salesperson, on the other hand, usually brings the sale to completion.

The demand for industrial goods tends to fluctuate much more widely with the ups and downs of the general economy than does that for consumer goods. This is primarily due to the relative durability of industrial goods (it is easier to extend the useful life of existing equipment and postpone purchasing replacements) and to the fact that the demand for industrial goods and services is dependent on other factors: the demand for consumer goods and services, and the state of business confidence about the present and future economic situation.

Another difference worth noting is that industrial purchasers buy products for their companies, not for themselves. Clearly it is sound buying policy for them to have several different sources of supply. Consumers may likewise spread their purchases among a number of different brands and/or sources of supply, but in their case the motives are likely to be inquisitiveness and the desire to experiment.

MARKETING RESEARCH

In many marketing activities, management wants to obtain certain data. Who will buy the product? What will they buy? Where will they buy? When and how will they buy? If valid answers can be found to these questions, the company has a very good chance of securing a footing in the market.

Marketing research can be briefly defined as the systematic, objective and exhaustive source of, and study of, the facts relevant to any problem in the field of marketing. However, the best way to appreciate the scope of marketing research is to consider its activities. These include the following:

- *analysis of economic trends:*
  short-term forecasts
  long-term forecasts
  general consideration of economic data
- *study of market structure:*
  population size, distribution, age, income levels
  structure of total market
  company's share of market
  competitors' shares of market
- *analysis of competitors' activities:*
  competing products and their prices
  competitors' marketing methods and policy
  distribution channels used by competitors

- *study of sales trends:*
  effect on sales of changes in selling and advertising policies and of any market occurrences such as import restrictions, expansion, etc.
- *analysis of profitability:*
  of markets
  of products and product groups
  of territories
  of wholesalers and retailers
  of sales force
- *analysis of distribution:*
  retail and wholesale distribution attained
  retail and wholesale distribution available
  rate of product flow along distribution channels
  handling and storage during distribution
  wholesalers' selling methods
  retailers' buying policies
  sales-force territories
- *studies of product and packaging:*
  physical performance during distribution
  performance in hands of consumer
  new uses for old products
  new product utility
  physical and psychological characteristics of packaging
- *determining consumer reaction and knowledge:*
  effect of price on demand
  use made of product
  opinion of product
  buying habits with respect to product
  opinion of advertising and themes
  opinion of company
  knowledge, use and opinion of competitive products
- *determining distribution-channel reaction and knowledge:*
  opinion of sales and credit policies
  attitude to product and to competitive products

opinion of company and sales force
arrangement of the selling situation

- *measuring advertising effectiveness:*
  media research
  copy research
  advertising-message awareness, perception and acceptability levels
- *estimating markets:*
  new products in new markets
  new products in existing markets

Clearly this great array of activities can be broken down into five main types of research:

1 *product research*—product and packaging, analysis of competitor activities, pricing profitability, etc.
2 *user research*—market structure, sales trends, consumer reaction and knowledge, etc.
3 *sales operations research*—distribution-channel relations, sales-force effectiveness, physical distribution, etc.
4 *communications research*—advertising effectiveness
5 *business research*—economic trends, economic data

All research projects should start with a clear statement of objectives. Field survey work can easily go off at an almost unlimited number of tangents if it is not geared to and controlled within set objectives. If the problem to be researched is stated only vaguely, or if the wrong problem is given, or if the reasons for the research and the uses to which it is going to be put are not made clear, then the researcher is going to have a difficult time designing an effective and efficient research plan. That may seem obvious, but it is surprising how often companies waste money through failing to brief market researchers properly.

Indeed, the key to getting the best out of a research company is correct briefing. The nature of the decisions with which management is likely to be confronted after the research has been completed must be in mind from the very start. Moreover, it is also essential that the research company knows the background and objectives of the client, as otherwise it has little hope of attaining a correct interpretation of the client's research needs. Without such knowledge, the research company could quite possibly produce results that were utterly irrelevant to the client's real problems. Nothing could be better calculated to induce in a client a lasting disenchantment with research! A simple but effective question to ask before a proposed market-research study is: 'How will the information gathered be used?'

Marketing research—procedures

There is hardly room within these pages to go into any great detail about the activities of the research consultant or company. Marketing research is a highly specialised operation. Anything more than a brief outline of the way researchers operate is a matter of purely academic interest to the average person in marketing.

In marketing research, no two clients' problems are alike, and neither is there any single typical procedure that is suitable for all situations. The following step-by-step account is applicable to most problems, but often some of the steps will be irrelevant. On other occasions there will be additional steps and/or different procedures:

- define both the problem and the objectives of the research study
- determine the methods for gathering primary and secondary data
- prepare data-gathering material
- plan the sample
- collect the sample
- tabulate and analyse the data
- interpret the data and prepare the report

By 'primary data' we mean data gathered specifically for the project in hand—for example, information gained from a questionnaire used in a face-to-face interview. 'Secondary data' is that already available from company, business, government or other records—for example, sales records or information from a government census.

There are three widely used methods for obtaining primary data: survey, observation and experimentation.

The survey method consists of gathering data by interviewing a limited number of people (a sample) selected from a larger group. Personal interviews, telephone interviews or postal questionnaires may be used over the sample. Although generally more costly than postal surveys or telephone interviewing, person-to-person encounters comprise the most efficient survey method.

The observation method uses no interviews. It merely looks at the way in which the target market behaves. The big drawback to this method is that it can tell only what *has* happened, not *why* it happened. It cannot investigate consumer habits and attitudes.

The experimental method has its main application in test marketing, whereby a 'control' market simulates an actual market situation. One of the major difficulties of test marketing is the selection of the control and test markets, and this is the main reason why the technique is not used extensively. Also, production runs and the economy of scale very often preclude the limited manufacture of a product for test-marketing purposes. Finally, test marketing is expensive and requires long, intensive work both in planning and in execution.

Qualitative research

Group interviews (or focus groups) can play an important part in marketing research. Essentially a tool of qualitative analysis, their most important role is that of providing better hypotheses for testing subsequent 'quantitative' surveys. Group interviews are frequently used at the planning stage of a quantitative consumer survey (using the conventional survey methods described above) and in motivational research.

In the former situation, the group discussion(s) focus the questionnaire onto those areas that are found to be the most important. As well as 'pilot testing' the questionnaire, the group discussion can assist in the understanding of the types of people who make up a particular market and the reasons for their buying behaviour. Group discussions entail fewer interviews and encourage the participants to stimulate each other in bringing forward ideas and relating their own experiences and impressions.

Group interviews and group tests are often used to determine the types of data which a more intensive quantitative analysis, based on a far larger sample, should seek. For example, a company which produced classified telephone directories believed that one aspect of these gave it an 'edge' over its competitors. Group interviews suggested that, while the public were aware of this aspect, they regarded it as of little importance. The company was able to ask the right questions in its much more wide-scale survey, and subsequently altered the theme of its advertising.

Advertising and advertising media research

To whom should the advertising message be directed? What theme should be used? Answers to the questions listed below provide advertisers with information about the target audience and the appropriate theme to use:

- What kind of people are the likely buyers for the product?
- Who will most strongly influence the buying decision?
- For what reasons do people buy the product? Conversely, for what reasons do people *not* buy the product?

The answers to such questions are obtained by the survey method. Such a thorough market examination is a prerequisite of any substantial advertising campaign. Motivation research – in that it seeks to relate people's desires, emotions and intentions to product features and communications material – also plays an important part in planning the advertising campaign by helping to suggest the most appropriate theme and the most appropriate presentation for the market.

Where and when should the message be delivered? Available statistics (i.e., secondary data) may often answer this question. Or, before planning the campaign's timing and delivery, it may be necessary to survey consumers' habits.

What media should be used? Media research aims to tell the advertiser whether or not the message is reaching a large number of potential customers at a realistic cost. Media research unearths facts relevant to such matters as the appropriation of advertising between North and South, town and rural, etc., the cost of achieving maximum coverage, the readers of morning newspapers who also read an evening newspaper, and so on. Again, available statistics can provide some of the answers. (Often these come from the publishers concerned: be cautious of biased presentation of statistics from this source.) Methods such as readership surveys and penetration surveys can also be utilised.

Which is the most effective presentation? Two of several methods used to measure the presentation of the advertising message are the controlled opinion test (a sample of consumers is shown a number of advertisements and asked to rate them for interest, eye-appeal and sales inducement) and the paired comparison test (respondents rate pairs of advertisements from each of the series to be tested).

Was the message effective? Once the advertisement has appeared, the advertiser and the advertising agency want to know whether it was read/seen and whether it was effective. Readership, recognition or recall tests can be used in order to determine whether the communications material was read/seen, what parts of the message were remembered and whether the respondent knows who the advertiser is.

Judging a marketing research report

The person who commissions marketing research is responsible for defining the objectives of the project and explaining the use to which its findings will be put. When the report is received it should then be checked to see that its findings are relevant to the terms of the enquiry.

The marketing research company has the responsibility of proving that:

- the right population was sampled
- the size of the sample was adequate to collect results of the desired accuracy

The research company should also:

- state the interviewing procedure and include a copy of the questionnaire used (if any)
- make available copies of interviewers' instructions and details of field supervision
- state the number of persons who answered each question
- point out the accuracy of major answers, so that the client knows how much reliance he or she can place on these answers

- state clearly the inferences that may logically be drawn from each set of answers
- state general conclusions and recommendations from its appreciation of the whole body of information gathered—although such comment should be clearly distinguished in the report from factual results

For a short time, the research company has been closer to the problem than has the client. Even if its general conclusions are not acceptable, its statement should stimulate the client to think further about the problem and the use to which the survey findings can be put. Successful marketing is derived as much from an attitude of mind as from the use of specific research techniques. Research cannot generate creative flair, but it can be used to check ideas that are not feasible or effective.

We can summarise by saying that marketing research:

- isolates the company's problems
- keeps the company in touch with its markets
- reduces waste in marketing methods
- can show the company where it is going
- can be used for advertising, sales promotion and merchandising purposes
- can develop new sources of profit through new markets, new products, and new uses for established or improved products
- can reduce production and administrative costs

4 PRODUCT PLANNING

The marketing-oriented company recognises that the key to its survival and growth lies in the continuous development of new and improved products. We live in an environment where the key to business success is the word 'new'. This is as true for service industries as it is for manufacturing industries. Peter Drucker, the eminent US business author, recognised the importance of the development of new products when he wrote: 'Because it is its purpose to create a customer, any business enterprise has two – and only these two – basic functions: marketing and innovation.'

Under modern conditions of competition, it is becoming increasingly risky not to innovate. Consumers and industrial users want and expect a stream of new and improved products, and your competitors will do their best to meet these needs. However, launching a new product has certain disadvantages. It involves risking money and it absorbs a great deal of management time. Some markets have proved particularly difficult for new products to penetrate. For example, it has been found that women are only too happy to try out a new shampoo, leading to high hopes on the part of the manufacturer, but are then content to revert to their original brand. The new shampoo must be identifiably better if it is to capture a share of the market.

Timing is a particular problem. Because a product fails at a particular moment does not mean it follows that it cannot succeed five years later or that it could not have succeeded five years earlier. Indeed, one of the better definitions of marketing is that it gets the right product, at the right price, at the right place, at the *right time*, and in the right light.

Obviously it is essential, if the new product is going to be successful, that its quality should meet market requirements. But this in itself is not enough. The marketer has to ask: 'Why should the consumer buy my product or service rather than what is already available? Why should the trade tie up stocks in this instead of, or in addition to, the existing alternatives?' Although it is quite possible for 'me-too' products to succeed on the basis that they offer variety, this will not necessarily happen in a developed and strongly competitive market—witness current disinvestment activity by conglomerates throughout the developed world.

Planning product strategy

Product planning is not something that applies only to new products. The introduction of new products, while of intrinsic value to the future growth and profitability of the business, must not be allowed to draw the company's attention away from the possible extension of the profitable existing products.

Dropping products

Most companies carry unprofitable products. If the sales of one product are independent of other products in the range, the decision is obvious: drop a product that is making no contribution to overheads unless there is good reason to believe that sales will pick up. That is the theory. The practical difficulty is that many companies do not know with any reasonable accuracy the marketing costs and the profit (or loss) contribution of their individual products, customers, sales territories or other segments of their business. Vested

interests, sentimentality and unfounded optimism can likewise cloud the decision.

When sales are interdependent, the decision to drop a product is more complex. Accurate costing can tell the decision-maker what a special high-prestige order, or low-volume line, really costs the company. It may well be that a seemingly loss-making product is in fact contributing to the company's profitability, in that it makes people more likely to buy the other products. Alternatively, the decision may be made to take the plunge and experiment by making some product lines unavailable to certain customers in order to evaluate what actually happens to sales. Such an experiment has to be carried out methodically, and the results must be analysed carefully. Some hard facts will inevitably emerge about the acceptability or non-acceptability of alternative company lines, and about the types of customers, if any, who are lost. There are many examples of a concentration on relatively few products and a dropping of others improving a company's profitability.

Perhaps the most important step for a company to take is to set up a methodical system for product-range review. The contribution of every product should be analysed by senior management at regular intervals.

Modifying existing products

A product modification is any deliberate alteration in the physical attributes of a product or of its packaging. Some products cannot be modified: the competition focuses on merchandising differentiation rather than product differentiation. However, most products are capable of substantial variation in their physical or functional attributes. A number of factors may prompt the manufacturer to alter the product. New technology may provide an opportunity for new product development. Modification may be a necessity because of the activities of the competition.

What kinds of product rejuvenation can we consider? The functional attributes of colour, size, material and styling—any one or a combination of these attributes could be candidates for change. Product modification involves risks. To lessen the risk, the old product may continue to be sold alongside the new. Most important of all is adequate investment in marketing research concerning the product and its market, so that better estimates of the sales impact of the proposed product modifications can be achieved.

Adding new products

The decision to take on a new product involves, at least in theory, the assessment of the net result on the company. The total position *with* the new product has to be reviewed against the total position as it would be *without* it. Overall strengths and weaknesses of the company need to be considered - does it have the financial strength, experience with raw materials and production processes, management skills, distribution channels, selling strengths, public acceptance, etc., which will be needed if the product is to be a success? Likewise, the question of company marketing objectives arises. The choice of new products needs to be made in the light of overall objectives.

A new product inevitably generates interest and excitement, and the bread-and-butter business of the company can collapse disastrously as the executives concentrate on planning the launch of a new line. Leslie Rodger in *Marketing in a Competitive Economy* (London: Hutchinson, 1965) has offered tentative generalisations as to the successes which some companies have achieved:

> These fall into three groups—those generalisations that can be made about the company itself, those that can be made about the product conditions which appear to be favourable to successful new product introductions, and

those that can be made about the market conditions for new products under consideration.

First, as regards the company itself, success seems to be more likely if (a) the company has a background of engineering, marketing and research knowledge, skill and experience in the product fields concerned; (b) top management gives adequate attention and priority to the new product programme; (c) the company has experience in the planning and management of test markets and in the analysis and interpretation of the results of test markets; (d) there is an opportunity to use existing facilities, resources and personnel in order to keep down the level of costs.

Second, as regards the product conditions favourable to successful new product introductions, these would appear to include (a) the necessity for having a new product which offers a difference which is of significance to, demonstrable to and preferred by a large enough group of customers (this is by far and away the most important source of a company's competitive differential advantage); (b) the necessity for providing an opportunity to create a difference in advertising and promotion (it is often possible to build into a technically undifferentiated product a genuine customer benefit which will serve to distinguish it from the competition and provide a basis for customer preference, e.g. a better or more convenient form of packaging, a better way of distributing and making the product available at a time and place more convenient to the customer); (c) the necessity for making a product that will meet a real need either not being filled at present or better than any competing products and that will sell in sufficient volume and provide a sufficient margin to pay for the promotional support needed to create sales.

Third, a new product, generally speaking, has a better chance of succeeding if (a) the market is an expanding one, and is broadly based across a large number of potential customers; (b) the market is going through a period of change; (c) there is a lack of strongly entrenched competition in the mind of the customer and therefore an opportunity to create a strong brand identity for the new product; (d) the competition is unlikely to be able to take serious counteraction quickly against the new product or the initiating company's established products; and (e) the market is relatively stable in the sense of being free from violent ups and downs of a general economic or seasonal nature.

Product evaluation

Many companies tend to launch new products as soon as they are available without doing much, if any, preliminary market evaluation. Such an approach can prove expensive and lead to the failure of the entire operation. A company should evaluate as early as possible the risk, the size of the opportunity, and the amount of innovation necessary in the market involved.

The company needs to know a great deal about the new market it wants to enter:

- Who are the potential customers?
- Where are they?
- How big is the estimated market?
- Are there similar products on the market?
- Who are the competitors?
- What sort of reputations do those competitors have?
- How do the competitive products compare?
- What share of the market do the competitive products hold?
- What will be the competitors' reactions to the appearance of the new product?

Consumer habits and attitudes need to be known. How frequently is the product purchased? Where and when is it purchased, and what are its most attractive (and least attractive) features so far as the potential consumer is concerned? What is the product expected to do? Does it have secondary (perhaps undesirable) uses? What are the best materials and equipment? Is there capacity available, or will new machinery be required? How long are delivery lead times? What will the rate of production be? Will the new product affect the production of existing ones? Has the product been costed accurately? What expenses will be incurred by product research, design and development, packaging, advertising and sales promotion, direct selling, installation, servicing, warehousing, transportation, and so on? What will the pricing policy be? What are the important factors relating to labelling and packaging? How will the product or service be sold? Can the existing sales organisation handle the new product, or will it need a separate or reorganised selling force? Will sales representatives need special training? What type of distribution will be used? Which distribution channels? Will additional warehousing facilities be needed?

The product will almost certainly require promotion. Should a launch campaign be planned? Which are the best media in terms of cost and the target market? When will you instigate the campaign and what will be its main message? Which supporting media will be required—point-of-sale material, merchandising, introductory offers, etc.? When and how will sales staff and distributors be briefed about the new product?

The product life cycle

As we have seen, products cannot hold their market position indefinitely: new items and lines are constantly being added and old ones dropped. The lifetime sales of products follow a typical pattern of development, known as the product life cycle. Virtually every product goes through such a cycle, although different types of products, according to their physical or 'personality' characteristics, have different life-cycle patterns, particularly with regard to their overall lifespan and the way that the cycle develops. Four phases in the cycle can be identified:

1 *Introductory phase.* This is the period during which the product is placed on the market. The phase covers the initial launch of the product, during which the awareness and acceptance levels are minimal. In this phase the product enjoys its greatest competitive differential advantage. The product should at some time during this phase – depending upon the level of investment – start to make a profit for the company.

2 *Growth phase.* The product begins to make sales gains as a result of the combined efforts of the various introductory promotional activities. Distribution is established and the emphasis is now on rapid market penetration. Reaction from competitors will heighten interest in both the product and its competitors, and market expansion can be looked for. As sales growth continues, a point is reached where further sales become progressively harder to achieve: there is a diminishing number of potential customers who remain unaware of the product. Pressure on promotional and distribution channels becomes greater.

3 *Competitive (or saturation) phase.* It is in this phase that sales reach and remain on a plateau marked by the level of replacement demand and by insignificant product differentiation. In order to create a differentiation and to lengthen the product's life, advertising and merchandising campaigns are launched to gain the attention of consumers and distributors.

4 *Decline phase.* Eventually sales begin to diminish as the product is gradually edged out by better products, by substitutes, or simply by a change of fashion. The manufacturer has to accept that the product will continue to decline until it

is completely uneconomic. It is now (or earlier, if the manufacturer has been able to identify previous signs of 'topping-out') that a modification or revitalisation of the product must be undertaken in order to adapt it to the needs of the market.

The implications of the product life cycle

The concept of the product life cycle has three important implications in terms of product planning. First, it illustrates that products have a limited life: even assuming that they go through a strong growth phase, they will eventually degenerate or disappear. Second, profits for the product usually follow a predictable course during the cycle. Profits are largely or completely absent in the introductory phase, tend to increase substantially in the growth phase, and start to diminish as the product moves into the decline phase, until they all but disappear. Third, the various elements of product planning assume different emphasis during the different phases. In each phase correct emphasis has to be given to marketing research, pricing, packaging, advertising, product improvement and other elements. And, at every phase of the product's life, the manufacturer must establish the balance of marketing ingredients to suit the particular circumstance in which the product finds itself in the market.

Organising for new product development

To ensure planned growth in the increasingly competitive marketplace, a company must have the right organisation to search for, evaluate and develop new products and to market them successfully. The development of new products is a major marketing function, and therefore a formal organisation responsible for this task is required. The functions of the new-products organisation are to be a focal point for new ideas, to evaluate those new ideas, and to make decisions about them.

The complexity of the organisation varies according to the size of the company—it could be one person devoting just a few hours of his or her time each week to the subject, or it could be a new-products committee that meets frequently. Regardless of the scale of the operation, the person or persons involved must be committed to specialisation in this area and must have a clearly defined responsibility within the marketing and company structure.

The basic responsibility areas of the product-planning organisation are:

- determining market needs and buyer habits and attitudes
- competitive intelligence
- determining optimum product mix over the number of product lines and the variations within each product line, and establishing the consistency of the products in accordance with the production, sales and distribution requirements of the company
- product evaluation—screening ideas concerning new products, improvements in existing products, and new uses for existing products
- product-feasibility tests
- product and packaging tests
- formulating marketing-strategy recommendations in relation to product development, packaging, price, 'personality', and so on
- preparing marketing-strategy recommendations in terms of timing and phasing for the product launch, sales and distribution plans, and the advertising and merchandising programme
- evaluation and regular review of the product-planning programme

Packaging in the marketing mix

A product's container or the way a service is packaged is an important factor in creating the correct image within the marketing mix.

Packaging must attract consumers, arouse their interest, impart information to them and encourage them to purchase the product. Packaging should be designed in terms of the market situation it faces and the functional constraints within which it will work. Often packaging is erroneously viewed as nothing more than a way of adequately protecting the product, and too little attention is paid to considerations of handling characteristics and appropriate sales appeal. Packaging must often meet the needs of a variety of marketing channels. Emotional as well as rational needs have to be recognised if packaging is to be an effective and flexible marketing tool.

Packaging need not be 'flash'. Indeed, in recent years a number of product lines have made a positive virtue out of the simplicity of their packaging. For example, although the savings involved in printing a single-colour label for a can of beans, as opposed to a full-colour one, are minuscule, the spartan nature of the label persuades customers that they are getting better value for money. They want good, cheap beans rather than elaborate labels. And the very simplicity of the packaging can in itself be eye-catching—especially when the products are seen *en masse*.

5 PRICING STRATEGY AND STRUCTURE

Pricing a product or a service is one of the most vital decisions made by management. Price is the only variable in the marketing 'mix' that generates *income*. All the others - product development, packaging, advertising, marketing, research and so on - generate *costs*. Pricing involves complexities that are to be found in no other area of marketing.

From a marketing point of view, the right price is the one that enables the best compromise to be made between supply and demand. From a consumer pont of view, value - and hence price - depends upon what the consumer is prepared to pay and upon no other factor. In other words, the *perceived value* of the product is the important point so far as consumers are concerned.

Pricing and marketing under conditions of

i *Perfect competition*

In this situation two conditions apply: there is a large number of small sellers and buyers, and the commodity is identical from whichever source it is bought. Thus price is the only factor to influence the market. Sellers accept the market price: if they overprice they will drive their buyers away, and there is no motive to cut prices because the commodity will sell just as well at the going rate. The closest approaches to perfect competition are to be found in fisheries and agriculture – for example, grain sales. However, perfect competition can occur in areas of business where price is determined by conditions outside the control of any one company.

ii *Imperfect competition*

In today's marketing environment, where most people live above subsistence level and exercise discretionary spending power, and where there are wide ranges of goods available from a diversity of suppliers, qualitative differentials become more important.

Economists tend to have a very simplistic idea of price. Their theory is that, when demand goes up, so does the price, and that when demand falls prices drop accordingly. Unfortunately for the theory, prices do not fall that easily.

There are a number of reasons why companies are reluctant to bring prices down. First, a reduction may simply encourage the competition to follow suit. A series of price reductions could launch a price war and disrupt the market. Second, there is the belief that demand is inelastic – i.e., that when prices go down the overall consumption is unlikely to go up very much, and almost certainly not enough to compensate for the decreased profit per item. Third, when demand falls, the financial department will probably insist that prices be put up, perhaps on the grounds that the rise will have little effect on sales volume. This is especially true if a product has a virtual monopoly of the market. For example, the cost of Letraset has risen dramatically over the years, but sales volume has been little affected.

Price changes and customer attitudes

Price changes are always difficult to make. The risks of making them are high in competitive markets. Often companies delay in acting because they feel that raising prices will affect sales to such an extent that profitability will actually decrease. Several methods can be used to assess the probable reaction to price adjustments:

- attitude surveys - actual field samples conducted using a statistically valid sampling procedure
- mathematical models constructed using significant and controllable socio-economic variables as a basis
- experimental pricing in limited test markets

Price reductions, on the other hand, may not always be immediately effective inducements to buy because:

- purchasers may suspect a corresponding drop in quality
- the product may be considered faulty or relatively unacceptable - i.e., purchasers may think the price has been moved because the product is doing badly in the market
- especially in industrial markets, buyers may regard constant prices as an indication of reliability in trading practices—i.e., frequent price changes may give the impression of financial instability
- even though customers may not have an exact knowledge of the price of a particular product, they may have accurate ideas of price zones—the ranges of the prices of similar competing products

Overall, reaction to price movements depends mainly on the buyers' awareness of price, the nature of the market (price sensitivity), and the degree of quality the product is perceived to have.

Demand

'The demand for anything, at a given price, is the amount of it which will be bought per unit of time at that price,' wrote F. W. Paish in *Economics: a General Introduction* by Frederic Benham (London: Pitman, 1955). Note that by 'demand' we mean *demand at a price*; the term has no significance unless the notion of price is either stated or at least implied. By 'demand' we denote something different from 'desire' or 'need'. In other words, demand is a measure of the usefulness a product has for a consumer or market—and price is only one aspect of this usefulness.

There are three main areas affecting demand. First come market considerations. Within this area there are several factors to take into account when looking at the future fluctuations of demand. There is the matter of the world's population. This is growing but mobile: by the end of the twentieth century 60 per cent of the people in the world will be urban. Then there is the increase in demand for disposable items: as earning power goes up, more people will want deferable items such as luxury goods and holidays abroad. A final market consideration is customer satisfaction. Consumers buy for many reasons - economical, sociological, psychological, etc. Current fashions, taste, social aspirations, convenience and moral issues - all of these influence buyers' behaviour.

The second main area is concerned with company and product (or service) factors. Demand for a product is strongly influenced by the attitudes potential purchasers have about both it and the company marketing it. Product or brand reputation and 'awareness' of the company are all important. Among other ways, a favourable image can be created through effective advertising. The term 'promotional elasticity' is used to describe the change in demand as measured against advertising expenditure.

Finally there is the question of demand for other products (services): this will affect the demand for a particular product or service. The reputation of competing products will influence demand, as will availability, aesthetic appeal, performance, and so on.

Pricing Policies

Market penetration

Under this policy, low prices are used to gain market penetration quickly, so that break-even point is reached as soon as possible. A market-penetration strategy may be used when the market is very price-sensitive, where large economies in production are gained, or in order to discourage competitors from entering the field.

Short-term profit maximisation

This strategy may apply where innovation or exclusiveness gives an initial advantage and where product life cycles are short (for example, in the field of fashion). This policy has occasionally been used to segment markets, to recover costs swiftly when the market has been perceived to be risky, or to compensate for high development costs.

Satisfactory rate of return

This policy is used when companies assess a reasonable rate

of return in relation to their investment and the risk involved. Target pricing is a more advanced form of the policy: it aims to achieve within a certain timescale a predetermined rate of return on investment.

Product-line pricing

This involves gearing prices to a range rather than to specific products, so that low-profit lines may be used to support high-profit items. The use of 'loss leaders' to stimulate purchase of associated lines (e.g., cheap cameras to sell expensive film) is common in retailing.

Cost-plus pricing

This policy is used by retailers and by manufacturing industries using their own standardised production where costs are relatively static and controllable. When considering cost-plus pricing a company needs to consider variations in margins. Cost-plus pricing varies according to the type of cost to which those margins are added. For example, the margins may be added to the direct production costs and calculated in terms of the average costs of distribution and the overheads. Or the margin might be added to the direct production and distribution costs so as to cover overhead profits. A third approach is to consider differential overheads (estimated overhead costs incurred as a result of taking on specified business) allocated to the total product, or product-group costs, with the added margin covering profit only.

Variable pricing

Here the idea is to maximise profits for products and services for which the demand differs at different times: hotel rates, off-peak electricity and vegetables are good examples. Different prices can be negotiated with individual customers, and they can be applied also for high-profit returns for special extras—for example, 'custom built' products.

Competitive-based pricing

The majority of companies do not set prices in isolation. Instead, they price to achieve an advantage. This strategy applies especially when markets are very competitive and there is relatively little product differentiation. It is of importance also in markets dominated by major companies which have the power to exercise some degree of control over material costs.

Bid pricing

This applies when contracts are awarded by, for example, governments and major industrial organisations on a tender basis. The objective is to try to establish the maximum price that will nevertheless be low enough to secure the business. Price tends to be the main consideration; quality often comes a poor second.

Pricing tactics and demand

Indirect pricing differentials

These are special non-price allowances, service provisions, etc., made especially to major accounts where product differentiation is narrow. Examples are margin guarantees, special credit terms and promotional advertising allowances. Also there is indirect price competition, which can include free trial offers, introductory offers and multiple packs.

Special promotions

These usually involve a temporary price cut. They may be used for several reasons:

- *Novelty appeal*. Here the price cuts attract increased demand: it may be difficult to return to the original prices. Promotions stress the novelty of the product and, if handled imaginatively, may achieve greater product differentiation.
- *Psychological advantage*. Promotions tend to give a more dramatic impression of price advantage than is actually justified.
- *Brand switching*. Through promotions, consumers will be encouraged to experiment with new products. A percentage of them will stick with the products and come to use them regularly.
- *Sales incentives*. Promotions give a company's sales representatives the opportunity to draw attention to the product. New stockists may be gained and shelf-space and special displays may be obtained when the representatives' efforts are supported by promotional material.
- Help to even demand. Promotions can be used to stimulate product sales in off-peak periods, so that the year-round demand is levelled out. This gives benefits in terms of both production and distribution.

Pricing and packaging

The trend towards the pre-packaging of consumer goods has

given rise to variations in the quantities sold in packs, size variations, etc. This fact can be used to play down price differences.

Overall pricing policy

Pricing decisions are never made in isolation. They are governed by company policy, by market and economic factors, and by the activities of the company's competitors. It is important to appreciate that price is only a part of the total marketing 'mix' while at the same time recognising it as the sole element of the 'mix' that generates income. When determining a pricing policy, a number of product or service criteria have to be evaluated. What are these?

Consumer acceptance

This is price-related—if only in the sense that it concerns the customer's conception of what the product ought to sell for in the market. On the whole, a low price is normally equated with poorer quality and a higher price with better. Too low a price can be just as great a danger to the consumer's acceptance of a product as a price that is too high, and the importance of price as a factor that affects consumers' perceptions of the worth of a product can never be overemphasised. So the first criterion is to establish which price segment of the market the product is to be introduced to—or, if there is more than one price segment, which and why.

Profitability

Pricing is the key to most commercial revenue, and it has a major influence on the level of profitability. Profit is, obviously, the difference between revenue and costs. The amount of revenue involved clearly depends on the number of items sold and the cost of each item. When a company attempts to establish the profitability of one of its products it must certainly consider the elasticity of the market, or the lack of it. There is no point in marketing a product cheaply if the demand will hardly be changed. Another point is that, while price is a vital part of a product's image, the consumer's perception of what constitutes 'good value' may bear no relation to the actual production costs of the item.

Distribution-channel acceptance

A third criterion concerns the distribution channel. Companies have to consider not just the ultimate price but also the distributors' price. If a product is being sold not directly to the consumer but through a wholesaler, distributor or retailer, the influence the pricing policies of these middlemen are likely to have on the acceptance of the product is obviously important. It is necessary to know how the distributive trade will accept the product in relation to its profitability. In a highly competitive environment, price can be used as a very strong weapon to 'buy distribution'.

Volume

The significance of price as a 'penetration' or 'skimming' device, or as a means of discouraging competition, relates to the overall volume of the market. Rather than defend itself from competition using the price 'shield', the aggressive company will use the price 'sword' to obtain sales volume and the profitability it desires. For example, Amstrad has cornered much of the UK market for wordprocessors purely because its machines are cheaper than those produced by its competitors. This has a synergistic effect: the more people using Amstrad wordprocessors the better sense it makes to have one, since it becomes more probable that one's clients will be using the same machine and the same software. Here is an example of the price 'sword' being used to carve out a new – and very profitable – market.

SELLING AND DISTRIBUTION

As we have seen, the functions of marketing are concerned with the development of a strategy that can be implemented through a number of tools. Some are concerned with finding out needs, some with ensuring that the product 'mix' and pricing are correct, and some with presenting the offering to the customer. In terms of the last of these, the simple matter of sales is clearly of major importance; sales have also a role to play in the other elements of the strategy. There are three main ways in which sales are effected:

- direct to the consumer
- through agents and wholesalers
- through retail outlets

To obtain distribution through one or all of these channels, the manufacturer has to establish the organisational needs of the sales force.

The size of the consumer or retail sales force depends on a number of factors, including the size of the company, the width, depth and consistency of the product or service mix, the numbers of potential outlets, and the level of the company's ambitions to distribute its products.

A common method of determining the size of the required sales force is the 'work-load' approach. Existing customers are grouped according to how big and/or how profitable they are, and a required level of annual call frequency is established. The number of accounts in each group is multiplied by the desired call frequency and this provides a figure for the total calls on existing customers per year. Then the total number of new accounts required per year is estimated, and a calculation made as to the average rate at which new (pioneer) calls generate new accounts. A grand total of required calls is now computed. The average number of calls a salesperson can make in a working year is calculated. From here it is obviously mathematically trivial to compute the number of people there ought to be in the sales force.

The structure of a sales force

The traditional method of structuring a sales force is by territory. This works well in companies with a homogeneous set of products and markets. The sales representatives' responsibilities are clearly defined, and it is easy to compare the performance of one representative with another. Travelling time – i.e., non-productive time – is cut to a minimum.

Alternatively, the sales force can be geared to product or service structure. This method is more applicable to larger multi-product companies, or to companies whose products are diverse and highly technical. One drawback of this method is that sales representatives from each product division travel over the same routes. However, the fact that each representative can become an expert in his or her particular product/service may more than make up for this by increasing the effectiveness of the time spent in the actual selling.

A third stratagem is to base the organisation of the sales force on the structure of the market, according to different types of customers, different channels of distribution, different individual customers, or different sizes of account. The system is most efficient when customer groups are clustered, as is usually the case in industry, because then the sales representatives rapidly become familiar with their customers' type of business and the problems involved in it.

Economics of the sales force

As we have seen, it is often difficult to assess the exact contribution and cost of each element of the marketing 'mix'. When it comes to selling in the field, however, one can to a very large extent make a meaningful measure of cost and performance. Here is a sample of the questions which must be asked if one is to attempt a valid evaluation of selling costs:

- Does the territorial distribution of the representatives accord with the distribution of sales potential? To put it more simply, are there too few representatives in regions where sales could potentially be very high, and too many in areas where one or two representatives could cope perfectly adequately?
- How are the sales organisations of your competitors territorially distributed, and why?
- Is business spread widely enough to avoid vulnerability?
- Conversely, is business *too* widely spread, so that there is overconcentration on accounts of small potential and comparative neglect of larger outlets?
- Is the present pricing system consistent with efficiency and cost-saving, or is it simply arbitrary? Are the prices given for quantity purchases related directly to delivery costs? Would it be possible to arrange for special terms on full loads delivered directly by the company, saving the costs of handling in the warehouse? What is the most effective system of regulating profit margins to wholesalers and retailers? (For example, you might have a two-layer system whereby there is one fixed price for retailers and another fixed price for wholesalers, regardless of the size of the order. Or you could base your price on the

quantity ordered of an individual product, or give a percentage discount calculated according to the monetary value of the total order.)

- What is the policy towards new accounts? How far should the number of new accounts be restricted, so that for each of them there can be adequate concentration on follow-up and development?
- What is the most effective and economic journey cycle? Should there be a standard frequency of calling, irrespective of the size of the outlet? Should the question of repeat calls be left entirely to the discretion of the representative, or should there be a general policy that certain types of outlets are to be visited more frequently than others?
- What records do representatives keep? Are they in fact necessary? What records and reports are vital for personal selling efficiency and management control?
- What can be done to improve the speed of cash recovery – in other words, to get people to pay faster?
- Are customers and potential customers classified by sales representatives and sales-administration personnel as effectively as they could be?
- Where are major sales expenses incurred? Have these been analysed sufficiently, and have any steps been taken to see if they could be reduced? What are the variations from district to district, area to area, and representative to representative? Are those variations justified?
- Is promotional material used efficiently?
- What types of sales aids could be introduced to improve the selling operation, and how can the expense be justified?
- How many accounts have been lost and *why* have they been lost? Does the company have any system of finding out why accounts are lost?
- Is the time between order and delivery satisfactory to the customer? Is the transport organisation being forced to deliver more swiftly than makes economic sense? Is the delivery-time of your company markedly superior or

inferior to that of its major competitors?

- What is the percentage of bad debts? What methods can be devised to improve credit control?
- Is it possible or desirable to make long-term contracts?
- What complaint procedure is used, and is it simple and effective?
- What arrangements are being made to ensure that the level of customers' orders is at least being maintained and preferably increased?
- Is it possible to train or instruct wholesalers' sales representatives better to sell your company's products to retailers? Could you offer effective incentives?
- Are there any systems to discover potential new customers?
- What is the turnover rate of the sales force? Does this vary according to areas? If so, why?
- Is the routing of the calls made by the sales representatives economically organised?
- What are the proportions of (a) interviews to calls, (b) orders to interviews, and (c) orders to calls? How do areas and representatives compare in these respects? Are there reasonable justifications for any variations?
- Are your sales representatives kept fully in the picture regarding essential developments? If not, what is wrong with your communications structure?
- How much time do district and area managers devote to continuous field training, and how much do they waste on unimportant clerical routines?
- How high (or low) is the morale of the sales force?
- Are sales representatives selling the advantages of the company's products or are they simply projecting their own personalities?
- Is the sales force too big or too small in relation to the capacity of the company and to the level of sales required if overall profitability is to be achieved?

Control of the sales force

Any sales force must use systems and adhere to them strictly. The reporting system, selling presentation and everything else integral to the field-selling operation should be systematised. Yet the systematisation must not be so involved that it eats into field-selling time, nor so complex that the sales representatives simply disregard it.

Selling is a lonely and hostile job. Sales representatives have to put up with many aggravations – sometimes from their own management as much as from their customers and competitors. They must have supervision. They need regular, close and systematic contact with their field supervisor or sales manager, who should be able immediately to interpret company policy and to answer queries and problems as they arise. Continuous guidance, regular contact with head office (both written and personal) go a long way towards ensuring that the sales representative is self-sufficient and self-reliant.

A sales force must be kept informed of what is happening in the market, in the company, and in every other aspect of business that might have relevance to its efforts. Such an information system has to be two-way. In terms of immediacy of information, the sales force is perhaps the best source of quick on-the-spot insight into the market. The sales force should regularly be given literature, personal encouragement and information about both the product and developments in the product field. Conversely, the sales force can be a most valuable source of ideas for product development, product variation and new forms of merchandising and promotion.

Selection of distribution channels

The selection of distribution channels is one of the most

complex decisions facing a company. Usually a range of alternative ways to reach the market confronts the company, each of those options likely to have an immediate effect on other elements of the marketing 'mix'. When selecting distribution channels a company should start by clarifying channel objectives, alternatives and likely returns. Marketing channels range from the simple to the complex. At the beginning of this chapter (page 71) we listed the various alternatives; here we go into them in more detail.

Direct to the consumer

Typical examples of this sort of distribution are companies engaged in the door-to-door selling of cosmetics and companies which sell their goods by direct mail order. This distribution channel is characterised by the absence of independent selling intermediaries (or middlemen) between the company and the buyer.

Through agents and wholesalers

The wholesaler's functions can be summarised as follows:

- financing stocks
- holding stocks
- servicing
- selling (prompting the retailer to stock and sell the merchandise)

The functions of the wholesaler are in essence the same as those of the manufacturer selling direct to retailers—except for after-sales service, which most wholesalers obviously cannot supply. This means that the wholesaling function can often be effectively performed by the manufacturer.

Agent-distributors are a slightly different beast. They

usually provide paid publicity and/or advertising, as well as a sales organisation and possibly also a service facility. There are various forms of agent-distributor with different ways of dividing the task and the cost of selling and of physical distribution between the agent and the manufacturer. The arrangement between manufacturer and agent-distributor usually involves an agreement concerning exclusiveness: the agent undertakes not to stock or sell any competing brand, and the manufacturer promises not to contract any other agency within that area or region to do so.

Through retail outlets

Here the middleman is the retailer, whose function is to purchase the company's products and re-sell them at a profit. For a great number of products, pre-selling and the directness of communication between manufacturer and consumer have changed the role of the retailer (and, for that matter, of the wholesaler, too). The emergence of supermarket chains and retailer buying groups, with the retailer able to act as a freelance merchant, is now forcing companies to try to arrange matters so that the retailer is virtually forced to stock the company's products. The company does this by establishing a strong brand loyalty with the consumer, using mass communications to establish a direct relationship with the consumer.

'The Trade'

A term used commonly in all sorts of businesses is 'the trade'. Inherent in the term is the belief that there is an orthodox method of distribution whose purpose is to achieve effective marketing. However, there may well be times when the company has to be imaginative and break away from orthodoxy. There is no place for middlemen unless they have a necessary function to perform, unless the margin allowed them is realistic (while giving them a fair profit), and unless they carry out their function in the intended manner. For various reasons, servicing and service requirements have changed, and they will continue to do so. With consumer goods, for example, servicing needs have become more complex because increased discretionary income has led to a greater consumer demand for convenience of use, product availability and improved product quality.

The established trade terms for any distribution channel are usually known, yet frequently they do not feature in the original costings of specific product lines with sufficient precision. Moreover, the possibility of varying terms is often not considered until sales have fallen below acceptable levels even though such a move, made early enough, could increase the flow of goods through the channel.

Decisions about distribution channels

The determination of distribution channels is influenced by a number of factors some of which are in the company's control and some of which are not.

Customer characteristics

When the number of customers is large, companies have to use long channels with diverse wholesale and retail intermediary levels. In addition to geographical dispersion and the number of customers, a further factor is the purchasing pattern of the buyers: having to fill small, frequent orders is tedious and far from cost-effective for a company, and so in such circumstances companies are likely to rely largely on wholesalers.

Product characteristics

Such product attributes as perishability, bulk, degree of product standardisation, service requirements and unit value have important implications when it comes to choosing the most suitable distribution channel.

Middleman characteristics

The strengths and weaknesses of different types of wholesale and agency operations need to be assessed. Middlemen differ in their aptitude for performing such functions as transit, advertising, storage and contact with retailers or resellers; also, they differ in their requirements for credit, the level of returns they anticipate, the level of training of their staff and their delivery. Additionally, the number, locality, size variations and functional capabilities of different retail outlet segments affect the choice of best distribution channels to use.

Competitive characteristics

In many industries the company wants its products to compete in or near outlets which carry competing products. In such cases, competitors' choice of distribution channels dictate those which the manufacturer would be best to use.

Company characteristics

The company's overall scale can determine the extent of its

markets and the size of its larger 'direct' accounts. Its financial strength will determine its reliance on intermediaries. The wider the product mix, the greater the ability of the company to deal with its customers directly. The greater the depth of the product mix, the more the company is likely to favour exclusive or selective distribution-channel arrangements. Another influence on channel preferences is, clearly, past experience of selling through different distribution channels.

Choosing among the alternatives

Manufacturers usually have a choice of many different distribution channels. The scope of the choice available can be evaluated according to various criteria:

- *Types of intermediaries*. In many industries, virtually all competitors use the same types of intermediaries, and so the company has few options about the sort of distribution channel it must use. In other industries, by contrast, competing companies use quite different distribution channels.
- *The number of intermediaries*. This is determined by the degree of market exposure sought. Companies producing convenience goods generally need intensive distribution, so that their products are stocked in as many outlets as possible. However, there are other approaches. Exclusive distribution is a policy whereby outlets are given exclusive rights to distribute the company's product in a particular territory. In granting exclusive distribution privileges, the manufacturer hopes both to gain a more aggressive selling effort and to be able to exercise more direct control over the intermediaries' policies on prices, credit, mark-ups, etc.

  Selective distribution is a little different. It involves the use of some but not all of the intermediaries normally available. Generally speaking, selective distribution enables the manufacturing company to gain adequate market coverage while at the same time allowing it more control and at less cost than would be the case had it opted for intensive distribution.

- *Terms and mutual responsibilities of manufacturer and intermediaries.* There are many possible variations of the mix of conditions and responsibilities (the trade relations mix) between manufacturers and intermediaries, and so the subject requires careful consideration. Pricing policy is a major element of the trade relations mix: discounts, parcelling, bonus offers and so on at different intermediary levels have to be watched closely in order to avoid discontenting one's middlemen. Conditions of sale relating to payment terms and company intentions to enfranchise other wholesalers are likewise important. It is worth noting that any intermediary will wish to receive full credit for all sales within their territory, whether or not they generated those sales themselves.

  In the case of exclusive and selective distribution channels where the relationship between company and distributor is close, it is likely that the nature of mutual services and the responsibilities of each partner will be comprehensive and well defined. Companies aiming for intensive distribution, on the other hand, may supply distributors only sporadically with such selling aids as promotional materials and services.

Distribution analysis

Distribution expenses account for a substantial proportion of total marketing costs. The objective, obviously, is to get the product through the pipeline to the consumer or end-user with the best possible service at the lowest possible cost. When trying to work out what the expenses of distribution are and whether they are justified, each product or service requires its own analysis: there is no universal golden rule.

The first considerations clearly are:

- the products themselves—their size, shape, weight, and so on
- the nature of the distribution—whether it is to be countrywide or focused mainly on specific regions, or perhaps on urban rather than rural areas, etc.
- the number of different types of customer to whom the products must be distributed (i.e., the market 'mix')

As with all aspects of marketing, it is important to keep an eagle eye out for changes in any or all of these aspects. For example, one company specialising in manufacturing cricket bats reckoned to sell them only to professionals. However, despite the fact that the bats were expensive, they were of such high quality that soon amateur cricketers, too, were wanting them. The company was clever enough to notice this at just the right time, and made the bats available through high-street sports shops. Obviously the company's distribution costs shot up, but this was more than compensated for by the extra volume of sales.

Other marketing factors have to be taken into account. For example, distribution costs should be included in the price the company charges for the product—either under manufacturing/supply expenditures or as a part of the overheads.

The particular sales tactics used for a product affects the distribution costs. To choose a single scenario by way of example, special offers or deals aimed at building sales volume can create peaks and troughs in the number of individual items of the product to be handled; similarly, they can present problems in terms of the build-up of stocks to meet hoped-for increases in demand. The same sort of problems are encountered whenever any short-lived product is introduced. If the projected increases in demand fail to materialise, additional costs will be incurred in order to clear the surplus stocks. Besides the possibility of error in the forecasting of peak or special sales, there is also the omnipresent question of the accuracy of routine sales forecasts: in either case, the greater the error, the likelier it is that stock levels will be larger than they should be. Only rarely do salespeople underestimate future demand!

Another marketing factor is the average size of each order. This is determined both by the types of customers served and by the number of end-users or consumers. These two factors influence the decision on the distribution channels to be used and therefore the costs of distribution.

Companies must modify their use of distribution systems and channels in response to changes in the nature of the market. Shifts in markets may be geographical, or there may be changes in buying habits or behaviour. In industrial markets, technological changes can likewise compel companies to modify their distribution methods.

Solving physical distribution problems is not just a matter of freight charges and stock levels: it requires an integrated approach, involving marketing and distribution operations and, if necessary, the other activities of the company. If the distribution problem is approached in this comprehensive way there is less chance that distribution costs will be simply a drain on the company's profits.

SALES FORECASTING

There are two possible bases for a sales forecast—what the product has done in the past, and what the market is expected to do in the future.

A sales projection, as a basis for producing a sales forecast, is obtained by considering the established market for a product (or group of products) in terms of past sales, and then extrapolating that trend into the future using methods as simple as putting a ruler across a graph, or as complex as 'exponential smoothing' or 'trend analysis'. The data used involve the rate at which the product has sold in the past, and the implied assumption is that all the factors previously operating in the market will continue to do so in the same way in the future. Projection is, therefore, essentially a short-term forecasting method, and it suffers from a general inability to anticipate market changes. Nevertheless, it is still a useful starting point for longer-term forecasts.

The longer-term prediction of market levels calls for more data and a greater understanding of the way in which a market operates. Instead of a simple calculation involving time and sales, an attempt is made to build a more comprehensive picture of the market by involving a number of marketing factors, including:

- the strengths of existing competitors
- the advantages of the product
- the marketing effort to be devoted to it

In every forecasting situation, realistic estimates of the strengths of the existing competitors have to be made. Competitors are rarely as strong as they seem: it is all too easy to make the mistake of basing your estimates on the superficial image the other company fosters. What matters most is not a competitor's managerial excellence but the number of customers with which it is in touch.

The advantages of the product are an aspect that may be given too much prominence, especially within a production-oriented company. Although it will almost certainly have its advantages, the product will quite probably have some disadvantages, too, and the temptation to ignore these should be avoided. The difficulty when weighing up the product's advantages (and the customers's recognition of this superiority and consequent readiness to pay a premium) and disadvantages (how many benefits will customers do without for the sake of economy?) is getting the right 'feel' of the market. Properly conducted research is useful—and is certainly better than relying on the tips about the market place passed back by the sales representatives.

Then there is the question of marketing effort. Predictions of sales are affected by the planned expenditure on promotion, whether on publicity or on field selling. In all aspects of promotion there are choices which have to be made and it is necessary to reach some conclusions concerning how the product is going to be sold. Current market practice should be assessed in terms of pricing, packaging, distribution channels, field selling, sales coverage, etc. It is important to consider whether the company should fall in line with the approaches of its competitors or take a completely new tack. For instance, if the competition is selling through retailers, could the product perhaps be sold direct?

It is traditional to consider the first year – divided into quarters or months – as the ideal short-term forecast period. The advantages of using a single year as a base period are, first, that we are conditioned to think in terms of days, weeks, months and years, and, second, that statistical data are normally generated in terms of those same time periods. However, there is no real reason why short-term forecasts should be based on a single year. Product launches commonly involve a three-year period. If it is known that operations are going to extend over longer than a single year, it can be a mistake to break up a forecast into one-year periods.

A true long-term forecast provides information for major strategic decisions; it relies heavily on trends. It makes no pretensions to accuracy, but seeks to indicate likely broad changes that could affect company operations. The main value of long-term forecasts is that they alert the company to those market or marketing factors which suggest that changes should be made to long-term objectives.

Forecasting methodology

There are two main groups of forecasting methodology—synthetic and analytical.

Synthetic forecasts are constructed from a number of individual reports—for example, the reports of company representatives. Such forecasts have the advantages that they use direct information and are easy to understand. Among their disadvantages are inadequate coverage, the lack of any estimate of their reliability, and the possible effect on them of individual bias.

In analytical forecasts, by contrast, total figures are broken down to reveal trends and random elements; these can then be recombined to give a projection into the future. Such methods are applied to time series (i.e., to one or more series of figures, systematically taken at regular intervals, relating to past performance) and are often described as 'time-series analysis'.

A time series rarely remains static: almost inevitably it shows an upward or downward trend. Such a trend will form the basis of the forecaster's decisions.

The trend must be examined carefully so that the forecaster is not misled by short-term variations from it. These may be either periodic or non-recurring.

The most important periodic movement is the seasonal variation—for example, sales of raincoats tend to drop during the summer. Other periodic movements are of a cyclical nature: they last longer than a year and usually do not exhibit the regular pattern of a seasonal variation. Non-recurring variations either are random and minor or relate to special promotions, advertising campaigns, etc.

The simplest way of analysing the overall trend is to look at the moving annual average. This involves examining the sales of the previous twelve months and then repeating the process monthly thereafter. The longer this goes on the simpler the analysis becomes, because in time it becomes possible to average out the figures for each twelve-month period. This sort of averaging eliminates the effects of short-term fluctuations and so allows the forecaster to detect the significant longer-term trend.

Where does all this data come from? As forecasters gather experience, they come to know which sources are best suited to their own requirements and concentrate upon them. The most profitable source of information is the company's own records. On a broader scale, government statistics are a useful source both of environmental market indicators as well as those relating to specific industries. Unfortunately, government statistics are often slow to appear, and so the forecaster has to turn to industry-sponsored research. Economic data are available *via* several business journals; data connected with individual industries are available through the respective trade, professional or industry journals.

We can summarise forecasting as follows:

Collection of information

- attempt to use as long a base as possible

- recognise that there is rarely, if ever, sufficient information available
- do not allow a lack of information to inhibit forecasting
- if direct information is not available, examine indirect possibilities

Analysis of trends

- attempt to use as long a base as possible so that you are not misled by short-term fluctuations
- eliminate false concepts by using constant values (inflation, seasonal trends, etc.)
- plot total trends
- examine trends for key variations
- analyse and assess total variations

Forecast of trends

- plot the total market growth expected
- analyse and assess the effect that expected changes in the economy will have on market growth
- analyse and assess current competition within the industry
- analyse and assess the expected competition for your industry's market

Forecasting and policies

- examine expected market share
- determine what action is necessary to increase your market share in terms of pricing policies, product mix, promotion and diversification or integrated vertical growth

Pointers

- forecasting is a continuous process
- forecasting always contains error, so recognise its existence
- if new information shows that the earlier forecasting contained an error, never allow it to stand—adjust your further forecasting according to the information, and tell everyone why you are doing so
- forecasting makes you think forward, and thinking forward can change the future

Estimating the market

Approaches to market estimation in any industry, or in any company, depend to a great extent on the nature of the product concerned and on the nature of the market. Three main approaches can be distinguished: the total market approach, the segmented market approach, and the residual approach. Each of these approaches allows projections to be made or predictions developed as a basis for forecasting.

The total market approach is concerned merely with total sales, making no differentiation between them, and hence is seldom applicable at either the market or the company level.

It is difficult today to think of any market in which both the nature of the product and the uses to which it is put justify a total approach: almost always there is some type of division of the market, either by product differentiation or by end-use. Such divisions necessitate the use of a segmented approach to the estimation of future sales and/or demands.

The interrelationship between markets that has to be taken into account when attempting sales forecasting can be exemplified by the way that the manufacturers of soap powders and detergents keep a keen eye on developments in the washing-machine market. The types of machines that are likely to be owned in the future can have a direct bearing on the types of soap powders and detergents that will be in demand.

Similar styles of market segmentation can be applied to ordinary consumer goods bought on a fairly frequent basis. One can examine, for example, the market in terms of different age groups or different areas of the country. Trends concerning sales of the different types of product, pack sizes, movements between price ranges, and so on, can be studied in considerable detail.

One type of statistical curve useful in the segmented approach is a chart of the product's life cycle (see pages 55–57), showing the introductory, growth and saturation phases. By studying a well developed curve in one part of the market one can often deduce the future progress of less developed curves in other sectors.

The residual method for forward estimation can be applied to a product which is mainly sold by the company in the year of its launch, but thereafter appears on the market a number of times before demand evaporates. The obvious example is the car industry. One approach to forecasting the market for new cars involves assessing the growth in the numbers of cars bought over previous years and predicting the future development of demand. Making appropriate allowances for scrapping, one can estimate the gap between the existing stock and the total demand, which gap will have to be filled by new car production.

Sales forecasting as a management tool

Sales forecasting is a management tool and serves a number of different purposes:

- It is the basis of the company's marketing operations; from it are derived sales and marketing budgets and estimated below-the-line expenditures. Within the company it may help planning if the sales forecast is broken down into sub-areas (covering products, territories, types of customers, distribution channels, etc.) and/or sub-periods (daily, weekly, monthly or quarterly).
- The short-term forecast assists production scheduling and stock control. The annual sales forecast, necessary for budgeting and profit-planning, relates directly to the company's financial and marketing activities.
- The long-term forecast is necessary if the company's requirements in terms of manpower, raw materials, plant and service facilities, and research and development are to be accurately assessed.
- It can be of importance in the setting of prices.

Reviewing forecasts

As we noted earlier, the sales forecast must be kept up to date. Adequate provision should be made for methodical review. The company needs to know about any internal or external factors that may affect the original forecast if it is to take full advantage of changed circumstances.

ADVERTISING AND SALES PROMOTION

So far we have discussed products, product range, pricing, and tools of selling and distribution. Each of these elements is a vital factor in the marketing 'mix'. However, a product may fail to sell simply because it is not being promoted to the right audience in the right way.

It is important to differentiate between advertising and sales promotion. As we noted earlier, advertising *pulls* the customer towards the product while sales promotion *pushes* the product towards the customer. For the overall promotion of a product to be successful, these two specialised activities must be coordinated.

Advertising has been described as 'mass selling', but the term is misleading: advertising's economics are mass and it uses mass media, but in fact it sells to people one at a time. Response to an advertisement, even though it may be appearing simultaneously in several million homes, is an individual concern, whether or not the individuals realise it. By contrast, the term 'sales promotion' embraces all the marketing activities other than face-to-face selling, advertising and public relations which stimulate customers to purchase and retailers to stock. Sales promotion therefore includes the production of point-of-sale material, the mounting of consumer and trade promotions, etc.

The development of the optimum promotional mix requires careful analysis of the value of each of the relevant tools—advertising, face-to-face selling and sales promotion. This has to be done relative to both the level of usage of each of them and the marginal effects of increasing the usage of one of them at the expense of another. The extent of these marginal effects depends upon the resources, problems and opportunities of the company. Two similar companies may well find that two quite different promotional mixes are most effective for them.

Depending on the product and on the market, the relative cost-effectiveness of the different promotional tools varies. An understanding of the comparative costs and capabilities of the various promotional tools is essential if the right sort of promotional mix is to be developed. The cost of an advertisement may need to be compared with that of a personal sales call. A high-risk product requires a high-calibre representative equipped with expensive selling aids, while a low-risk product, conversely, requires merely 'order-takers', but backed up by solid advertising. To put this another way, the shorter the selling chain, the greater the need for the sales representative; the longer the selling chain, the greater the need for advertising.

Advertising is probably the most cost-effective promotional tool in terms of creating awareness among the potential consumers. On occasion this can be done without even mentioning the product's name: successful campaigns advertising, for example, drinks, cigarettes and books have been run in this way.

The nature of the product, the stage it has reached in its life cycle, the buying process, the promotional strategy of the competitors—all of these factors are among those that affect the development of the promotional strategy. The matter of time is important, too. The promotional tools to hand, whether short-term and tactical or long-term and strategic, must be coordinated: immediate and specific objectives and broader, longer-term, strategies must be clearly established.

Advertising

Management has to have a clear understanding of exactly what it wants to achieve through advertising—through the overall advertising effort, through a particular advertising campaign, or even through a single advertisement.

Advertising goals should be as specific as possible. The more specific the goals, the better they can guide the advertising team to develop an effective message, to select and schedule media, and to measure advertising effectiveness.

Advertising objectives can be grouped under three broad headings:

1 *Consumer advertising objectives at consumer (or end-use) level*—for example, building awareness of the product or service, building familiarity with a pack or product.
2 *Consumer advertising objectives at trade level*—for example, building the morale of the sales force, building acceptance of the product within the distribution channels.
3 *Industrial and trade advertising objectives at industry and trade level*—for example, persuading a prospect to ask for a demonstration, pre-selling a product to its distribution channels.

Setting advertising objectives should not be confused with determining advertising methods. 'Increase consumer awareness in the market through saturation TV' is not an objective. Rather, an objective should be *measurable over a period of time*—for example, 'To increase overall consumer awareness of 'X' from the 5 per cent currently held to 15 per cent in the (target) market, defined as women aged 25–34 with school-age children, within a (specified) family income group, living in (specified) geographical areas, and to do so by a (specified) date.'

Setting the advertising budget

Unfortunately, there is no simple system of determining how much of the company budget to allocate to advertising. Those companies which do make a calculation of their advertising budgets commonly use one of the following factors as a basis:

- a percentage of last year's turnover
- a percentage of next year's anticipated sales
- a percentage of profit
- keeping up with competitors
- the objective and task method

Advertising expenditure must be related to the marketing and advertising objectives which the company aims to achieve. Any marketing plan designed to achieve these objectives will highlight strengths and weaknesses in terms of the product, the buyer, the competing products, and the marketing activities of the competition. Each of these elements will influence the size of the advertising appropriation in relation to the requirements of the overall promotional mix.

Percentage of last year's turnover

Basing the advertising appropriation on a percentage of the previous year's sales can be advantageous where advertising is a large part of the selling cost, where demand is known to be limited, or where production capacity is more or less inflexible. However, the calculation presupposes that the company has sufficient experience of advertising to the particular market to know what the actual percentage should be. The use of this method makes no provision for growth or for any rise in the cost of advertising. However, it can at least ensure that expenditure does not exceed earnings.

Percentage of next year's anticipated sales

With this method, the difficulty again lies in assessing a viable percentage. Additionally, basing the calculation on forecast sales is fraught with potential dangers, because it yields a larger budget when times are good and a substantial sales increase is anticipated, and a smaller one when times are tough and greater effort is needed to reach a given sales target—the opposite of what is required.

Percentage of profit

This method has more to commend it than do the previous two methods. However, there is no assurance that a calculation based on profits will bear a true relationship to the requirements of the marketing plan.

It also relegates the advertising appropriation *and* the expected profit to the bottom of the priority list, so that one can only be increased at the expense of the other.

The potential danger of such a procedure becomes evident if you consider two extremes. First there is the manufacturer who believes that the sales effectiveness of advertising is minimal and who, after a bad year, slashes the advertising appropriation in order to make a bigger profit in the next year. The other side of the coin is the manufacturer who expects miracles from advertising and continues flat out even when a credit squeeze or other circumstance has, at least temporarily, dried up demand.

Keeping up with competitors

If every company divided its advertising appropriation on the follow-my-leader principle the effect would be highly inflationary, with companies spending progressively more and more on their advertising. This alone is sufficient to show the weakness of this method—apart from the fact that the appropriation will obviously be unrelated to any overall marketing plan. It is nonetheless advisable to study the competitors' advertising expenditure when working out your own: you may well learn something.

The objective and task method

The most rational approach to assessing the advertising appropriation is undoubtedly the objective and task method. Rather as in product costing, it means itemising and building up rather than starting with a lump sum appropriation and then breaking it down for dispersal among the various channels of advertising. The different factors that have to be taken into account are normally considered in a sequence much like the following:

- The markets—how many different markets are there, what are they, and how big are they?
- The products—to which market or markets should each be promoted? Should they be advertised individually or can any of them be effectively advertised in groups? What is the profitability of each? Are any of the products new? (Usually more advertising is necessary for new products than for established ones.) What is the competition? At what buying level or levels should the advertising for each product be aimed?
- Communication objectives—what should you be saying, how should you be saying it, to whom, where and how often? The answers to these questions will influence your choice of media, size of advertising spaces, use of colour, etc.
- Company advertising—is there a case for a corporate campaign (i.e., to establish the image of the company as a whole)?
- Media—what media should be used to reach each market and buying level for each product or product group? What

would be the best media for a corporate campaign? In terms of the press you have to establish which newspapers and/or journals are appropriate, the number of insertions per product or product group, the size of the insertions, whether you should use black-and-white or colour, how many different advertisements you will need, and how large the costs of physical production will be. If planning to use television or radio, you have to think in terms of which areas, how many spots, and the length of the campaign. Direct mail involves consideration of the number and nature of shots, the size of the mailing lists, and the costs of printing, despatching and postage. Other possibilities include exhibitions or trade shows (allowance for stands and incidentals), distributor display material, films, videos and, of course, hoardings.

- Print—as well as printed material for direct-mail selling, you will need folders, brochures, catalogues, price lists, etc. Approximately how many of each will be wanted, and how much is all this likely to cost?
- Reserve for contingencies—to the figures calculated for predictable expenses needs to be added a sum to cover the 'extras'—advertising in special supplements or features, possible product changes, research on advertising effectiveness, and so on.

Apart from public relations, which normally cover the company's activities as a whole and are not considered in the advertising budget, projected advertising costs should be worked out for each product or product group, and then the totals added up. If the resulting sum is greater than what the company thinks it can reasonably afford, then obviously there will have to be cutbacks—but only on the basis that the task the advertising is expected to perform is reduced proportionately.

The advertising message

The advertising message has to:

- inform prospective purchasers about the product or service, its name, its function, its attributes, its price and where it can be bought
- persuade prospective purchasers that they do need the product
- persuade prospective purchasers that they should buy *this* product in preference to others

To the maximum extent, this informing and persuading should be related to the outlook of the individuals in the target market. People need to be able to identify themselves with the product: advertising is most effective when it both informs by telling people what they want to know and persuades by telling them what they like to hear.

Clearly we all share some unconscious mechanism which evaluates everything that we hear or see and classifies which things are worth our conscious attention and which are not. This 'screening' affects all our senses. Gaining attention is the first aim of any advertisement: obviously an advertisement which fails to attract the attention of a large proportion of the target market is likely to be a waste of money. Researchers into advertising effectiveness have worked hard on the measurement of 'attention value'. The problem is that their tests cannot accurately portray the level of the reader's attention at *the actual time of reading*.

Does it matter whether the advertisement is liked or not? Research evidence shows that in general likeability is not an important factor in an advertisement's effectiveness. For example, many years ago a major brewing company ran field tests of a television advertisement for a new beer it wished to launch. Questioned afterwards, the trial audiences said that they had enjoyed the advertisement; however, when interrogated further, the vast majority of people in the sample audience admitted that they could not remember the name of the product. Needless to say, the company adopted a new advertising approach.

And what of 'interest'? Instruments such as psychogalvanometers and cameras (to measure pupil dilatation) have been used to measure how interested test subjects are in advertisements presented to them. Here there are two aspects of particular note to the advertiser. Firstly, there is *stimulation*, represented by such advertising descriptions as 'startling', 'novel' and 'exciting', and secondly there is *enjoyment*, represented by such descriptions as 'entertaining', 'pleasant' and 'amusing'.

Overall, research suggests that there is something in the view that advertisements, to be effective, should expect some sort of contribution from the audience: if people can be induced to see things for themselves they are more likely to be compliant than if they are passive spectators. For similar reasons, if consumers can identify with the people or situations shown in the advertisement, the chance of persuading them to buy is greatly improved.

Media selection

The selection of the media in which to advertise depends on at least three factors:

1 The target audience's media habits,
2 The media's likely effectiveness in presenting the product,
3 Relative costs of the major media categories.

The relationship between media selection and the preparation of the advertising message is a chicken-and-egg one. On occasion the media plan is determined very largely by the needs of the creative people; conversely, the creative people often have to follow a pattern determined very largely by the media plan.

The media plan is a crucial part of an advertising campaign. The planner's job is to advise how to convey the message to the target market most effectively and most economically. Media selection is a specialised skill, and is usually provided to companies by their advertising agencies. In this book we have space for only a brief list of media attributes:

Television

- penetration into majority of homes
- generally less flexible than newspapers
- ideal for 'demonstration' of a product
- personal 'in-home' involvement
- cost per thousand consumers contacted above that for radio but below that for newspapers
- available every day of the week
- transience of message

Newspapers

- penetration into majority of homes
- geographically flexible
- good for pack establishment or identification
- good for extensive product description
- high cost per thousand consumers contacted
- available every day of the week

Periodicals

- penetration into (possibly) a high percentage of homes
- coverage is generally national
- medium cost per thousand consumers contacted
- there is usually the option to advertise in full colour

- length of reading-time: people may hang on to journals for months, whereas newspapers are normally thrown out the following day

Radio

- penetration into a very high percentage of homes
- transience of message
- opportunity to repeat the message frequently during the day
- geographical flexibility—you can choose exactly those parts of the country in which you want to advertise
- personal 'involvement' on the part of consumers
- lowest cost per thousand consumers contacted

Media strategy

The selection of the media to be used for advertising and the overall planning of the advertising campaign both have to be based on hard data. The media planner (assuming the company has one) needs therefore to be extensively and properly briefed. A reasonable briefing should include the following:

- basic information about the client for whom the advertising schedule is required
- the amount of money available for media advertising, as distinct from production or other charges
- the period that the advertising appropriation is intended to cover
- the campaign period: what is the starting date of the marketing campaign and how long is it going to last? (This must not be confused with the appropriation period.)
- how is the market for the product defined in terms of age, sex, geographical location, occupation, etc.?
- timing - when do buyers make their purchases, and how

often? Is the product bought on impulse or only after serious consideration?

- is the campaign concerned with the launch of a new product or is it a reminder campaign for an existing product or a holding campaign in a declining market? In which sections of the market should the campaign be intensified? What are the sales areas, and when do the sales drives (if any) start in each?
- are any groups (e.g., retailers, company representatives) singled out for special attention?
- what do the creative people involved in your advertising need to know in terms of media constraints the atmosphere required for the campaign (prestige or hard-sell), and so on?
- what campaigns (and how major) are your competitors mounting? Which areas are they operating in, which media are they using, and what message are they putting across?

Once he or she has the answers to all these questions, the media planner can then select the media most appropriate to the target market, the planned budget, and the weight of the schedules.

Media scheduling

The scheduling of the advertising carried out through the year or the campaign period can make a crucial difference to the total impact achieved. There are three basic elements:

- extent of coverage
- size of space (or duration of time)
- frequency and timing of insertion

Within the limits of the advertising appropriation, these have to be balanced against each other in whatever way seems best for the particular product and its market.

The juggling of the limitless variables available is, again, the responsibility of the media planner. However, it may be useful to include here the conclusions arising from psychological research in one study of the relation between repetition and learning:

- generally speaking, the greater the number of repetitions the better the retention
- a residual amount of learning always remains for a long period of time, but forgetting is very rapid in the period of time immediately after learning. Information learned more quickly is retained better than information learned more slowly
- repetition beyond the point needed to retain makes possible longer conscious memories

Measuring advertising effectiveness

Analysing the effects of advertising in isolation from other aspects of the marketing mix is almost always impossible; even when it can be done, under limited test-market conditions, extrapolation into larger areas cannot be guaranteed to produce reliable results. However, it is necessary to assess the success of any campaign in order to learn lessons for the next one.

No positive research techniques exist: established methods are useful to only limited degrees. Most researchers today agree that advertisements or campaigns can be satisfactorily tested, with varying accuracy, for certain criteria: how much attention the campaign attracted, whether it was accepted sufficiently to cause changes in behaviour or purchase, and whether or not it was understood. These are, of course, the same criteria as should have been used when developing the campaign in the first place.

At present the effects of advertising can best be measured

by assessing attitudes, knowledge of brand images or claimed changes in behaviour, using sampling done before and after a campaign. Researchers are rejecting the validity of certain criteria for this form of assessment. The first to suffer has been how memorable advertisements are, because there is no certain link between consumers' remembrance of an advertisement or a campaign and their subsequent pattern of sales purchase. In fact, remembrance of a creatively outstanding advertisement may have a reverse effect on sales. For example, many years ago a campaign on British television for a brand of cigarettes used a catch-line so memorable that it drove the brand right off the market: when people bought the product in the shops they were often teased by other customers because of the catch-line, and so many of them shifted brands. Similarly, an advertisement's credibility and apparent conviction have been found to have little bearing on what people actually buy. The consumer certainly does not have to *like* the advertising to buy the product.

The client-agency partnership

An advertising agency is a consumer/market-oriented organisation specialising in the field of creative communication. Provided the agency is given confidential access to all aspects of the client's business that have marketing relevance, it can offer practical help and advice over a wide range of marketing problems. The agency's involvement on a continuing basis in the client's basic marketing thinking and planning offers greater stability in the client-agency relationship. Likewise, it increases the agency's ability to produce more effective advertising.

The following are ten key factors in the client-agency partnership:

1 The successful client/agency relationship has many foundations, but the foremost is complete mutual trust. No

one aspect of the relationship tests that basic trust more than the transfer of information. Do not make the mistake of telling your agency as little as possible and expecting a decent result. The more input you provide the better the finished product, and a lot of valuable time and money will be saved achieving it.

2 Clearly define a formal system of contact and approval. Establish the lines of communication and tell the agency who has responsibility for the eventual approval of the advertising. Also, explain who has authority to demand changes in advertising plans or material during the stages before final approval.

3 Ensure that in the above system there is informal monthly contact with the agency at your highest marketing management level. At lower levels, contact should be much more frequent, so that the agency can be kept completely up-to-date with your thinking. The primary purpose of these meetings should be quite clearly understood: they are for *communicating information*, not for constantly amending instructions.

4 Insist that the account manager within the agency be fully involved in the campaign. Higher-echelon personnel, especially the person who captured your account, otherwise tend to become elusive, so that you are left dealing with a much more junior person.

5 Ensure that the agency does not try to sell your company more services than you actually want. And be wary of the agency that pretends to offer a special service or particular specialist skill which is in fact subcontracted out or given to another agency over whom you have no control. Be particularly sure that the agency does not put out creative work. If it does, it's a client, not an agency—and you are the one who is supposed to be the client.

6 Ensure that the agency is committed to your company, that it knows your markets and your products thoroughly, and their relation to each other and to your whole operation. Also, make sure the agency shows a sense of proportion in

dealing with different aspects of your company.

7 Be *involved* with the agency. The agency can never know more about your business than you do; conversely, the agency should not have to waste time and money finding out something you could readily have told them. You must be willing and able to get on with agency personnel at a personal level. In addition to being in frequent personal contact with members of your company, the agency must be seen to have an emotional investment in the relationship by showing concern for the company's welfare and getting involved in its activities. Never allow the situation to degenerate to the stage where you are having to spend much of your time keeping on top of the agency or simply keeping its personnel on their toes.

8 Prepare written briefs. Set out very clearly your policy in relation to a product, and provide the agency with all the relevant information you have. This should include, for example: the product profile and the relative importance of the product in relation to the rest of the company range; your marketing objectives; and background details concerning the competitors, the market, and your selling and distribution activities.

9 To maintain your good relationship, regularly evaluate the agency's performance. The evaluation should be both quantitative and qualitative - see checklist which follows:

CHECKLIST: EVALUATING AN AGENCY'S PERFORMANCE

Quantitative

- *Media buying effectiveness*—How effective is the agency in getting to the target audience, as often as possible, at the lowest cost?

- *Predicted achievements against actual costs*—Quantify and record sales volume or other current levels of awareness of attitudes concerning your products before a new advertising programme is initiated. Determine that it is feasible to create advertising which, supported by your other selling/marketing operation, will increase the above levels within budget constraints. Measure the results of the programme after a long enough period of time for any impact to have become manifest, and compare the results with earlier quantified levels.
- *Agency size*—Is it the right size? How big is your account compared with those of other companies the agency handles? Is the agency the right size in terms of keeping up with you?

Qualitative

- *Creative ability*—How productive of ideas is the agency? How high is its level of creativity?
- *Trustworthiness*—Can the agency be relied upon to pursue your interests with integrity and without frequent checking?
- *Honesty and courage*—Is there a willingness to stand by advertising ideas even if they are incapable of proof?
- *Understanding*—Is there a really close understanding of your business?
- *Enthusiasm*—Is the 'chemistry' right? How enthusiastic is the agency? Are the people there the kind who can work with and be acceptable to members of your company?

10 Be a 'good client'. Prepare thorough, detailed and clear marketing plans. Stay with your plans *and* your budgets. Have your advertising plan approved well in advance of individual campaigns. Allow the agency to provide its own creative guidance. Do not direct the way creative work is to be done. Encourage agency personnel to travel—to make field trips, meet distributors, attend sales meeting, etc. And pay the agency's bills promptly!

Advertising agency selection

Questions a company might ask itself when selecting an advertising agency would include the following extensive list.

Agency personnel

Do the knowledge, experience, personal ability and sensibility of the agency executives impress you? What is the extent of the participation of the top management and talent in client service? How many people does the agency have, and what is their ratio of staff numbers to accounts handled? Is the agency's organisation chart available?

Agency philosophy

Is the agency philosophy concerning advertising sound and convincing, and does it appear to offer a flexible approach to the problems of its individual clients? Does the agency specialise in certain types of accounts, or in types of services that are of particular interest to you? Is the agency a member of professional organisations—and, if so, what are those organisations?

Financial stability

Who owns the agency? What are their financial backing/ affiliations and credit rating?

Domestic and international organisation

Where is the agency's headquarters and where are its branch offices? What overseas connections does the agency have?

Account team

Who at the agency will make up the team working on your account? Indeed, will it be a team or just a one-man band within the agency? (In other words, how much time will be available for you?) Do the team members impress you in terms of their knowledge and experience of the advertising business? And do they impress you in terms of their personal ability and sensibility? Does the agency's approach to client service suggest that your account will receive fast and efficient servicing?

The agency presentation

Was there a person present who would be capable of controlling your account, and what was your reaction to that person?

Marketing capabilities

What evidence does the agency show of sound marketing thinking? What members of the team have previously worked in marketing management as advertisers? How capable is the agency to convert your marketing strategy into a workable advertising plan? If marketing services are required, is there evidence that the agency could do this effectively? Has the agency a high degree of integrity in deploying the marketing budget relative to its planned expenditure on advertising and promotion?

Creative and media philosophy

How can the agency's creative and media philosophy be adapted to relate to your business, your industry and your market?

Current accounts

What kind of accounts does the agency mostly handle? What current accounts does it handle? Is the agency too big, so that your company's account will come low down on the list of priorities? Is the client list impressive? How big are the existing accounts? Does the agency hold any of your competitors' accounts, and is this a matter for concern? What evidence is there of success with current accounts in terms of sales results, share of market, product acceptability, etc.? Will the agency be able to keep up with your company?

Account turnover

To what extent have accounts been lost or held? If many have been lost, why? Has the agency grown as a result of the increasing size of the accounts it handles or through gaining new accounts?

Demonstration of creative flair

Does the specimen promotional material produced for you by the agency suggest top creative flair?

Demonstration of media-buying efficiency

What media-rating services are used by the agency? What evidence is there of media-buying efficiency? Is the agency prepared to work with a media-buying service if required? What media research is purchased by the agency? What examples are there of media research commissioned by the agency on its own behalf? Or for clients?

Production facilities

Is the agency well organised in terms of producing material for press, television, radio and print? What are its facilities for the creation or purchase of production materials? Do the agency and/or its suppliers quote accurately, and are their delivery dates reliable?

Market-research facilities

Do the agency's internal research facilities have the ability to gather and analyse marketing information? What evidence is there of the agency having recently used market research from external suppliers (research agencies) conducted for clients?

Advertising research

What evidence is there of changes having been made to advertising copy as a result of testing? How interested is the agency in research into the effectiveness of communications?

Commission arrangements

What are the nature and extent of the services to be provided in return for the agency's commission?

Charges and fees

What is the agency policy on the charges they pass on to the client for creative work, production work, public relations, market research and other work it has commissioned from outside suppliers? Does it do so 'at cost', or does it add a profit margin? What is the agency's policy on fees for special assignments, marketing planning assistance, expenses, etc.? What are its terms of business?

Sales promotion

Sales promotion is the link between the face-to-face selling done by the company's sales force and the advertising directed to the customer. It is used both by the company and by its distributors. It works in three areas:

- consumer promotions
- trade promotions
- point-of-sale display

Within these broad categories there are many different methods of sales promotion. A selection of these is discussed below.

Consumer offers

The objective of a consumer offer is to secure customer trial and/or re-trial in the hope that brand loyalty will develop.

Free samples

This is one of the most efficient ways of launching a new product—but it is not cheap. The key things to keep in mind when you are considering a sampling exercise are that you should know why you are sampling and who you are sampling, and never attempt to save money by making the sample too small; for example, a single cup of instant coffee is unlikely to persuade the consumer to change his or her buying habits, but three or four cups of the new brand might well do so. Sampling should be carried out using the standard product; the packaging should conform to that used when the product is offered for sale. Otherwise consumers are less likely to identify the pack easily and positively when next they are shopping for (say) instant coffee.

Coupons

Giving consumers coupons to encourage their first or next purchase is an effective way of ensuring that at least some of your potential customers will try the product. However, it is once again an expensive business, and it is much more difficult to analyse the results than if you were giving out free samples.

Banded packs

This technique involves, for example, banding two identical packs together and selling them for a price less than the combined price the two would have if sold individually. Banding can also be used to assist a product launch: a pack of the new product (at a reduced price or possibly even free) can be banded to a pack of a successful established product. As a technique, banding has the advantage that the costs of such a promotion can be determined as soon as it has been decided how much of the product is going to be sold in this way.

On-pack offers

Using this promotional technique, an item may be attached

to a product which may or may not have direct relationship to that product—for example, a free comb might be attached to a pack of a hair colourant.

Trade offers

A trade offer normally has as its objective either a general widening of distribution or an increase in the level of stocks held by the trade customers; sometimes the aim is to encourage wholesalers or retailers to display the product more prominently, or to make greater use of display material. It normally takes the form of special concessions intended to induce the re-seller to buy in at higher levels than would otherwise be the case. Discounting to re-sellers is a sales-promotion technique that often gives much greater benefits to the manufacturer than would price-cutting at the retail level.

Packaging

Product or pack designs can, with a little forethought, often become the basis of future advertising or sales promotion. At the time when the design of the package is being finalised, the sales promotion and point-of sale considerations should include:

- is the pack easy to store?
- will the pack fit easily into existing racks, shelves, etc.?
- is the design of the pack such that, if later you want to add promotional messages, there will be no clash with the general image of the product that you wish to convey?
- is it possible to build into a product's pack features that can later be exploited in advertising or sales promotion?
- are the design graphics such that the packs are suitable for display *en masse*?

Point-of-sale display

This is a major tool of sales promotion when a product is usually bought on impulse rather than as a planned purchase. The use of point-of-sale material can be characterised by its four basic applications:

1 supporting a sales-promotion campaign
2 supporting a television or press campaign using theme-oriented material
3 as a merchandise carrier (e.g., dumpbins)
4 as retailer price tickets, etc.

If point-of-sale material is to do its job, the company must ensure that:

- a continuing study is undertaken of the outlets for which point-of-sale material is specifically intended
- the planning of point-of-sale material is part of the overall marketing plan
- the point-of-sale material and its design are integrated with advertising, packaging, promotional and distribution objectives
- where possible, creative ideas are submitted to a preliminary test before substantial expenditure is incurred
- the sales force is briefed and the idea is sold to them

See checklist on page 118 for a useful checklist concerning point-of-sale material.

Exhibitions

Exhibitions offer the opportunity to attract interested potential customers into an environment where a product or service can be demonstrated most effectively and at some leisure. Success involves detailed planning. An objective should be set and the main message to the customer and the terms of service on offer must be established. The stand design, the briefing of the stand manufacturer, the items to be displayed, the materials required, staffing and training—all need to be planned to a rigid timetable.

CHECKLIST: POINT-OF-SALE MATERIAL

- Has the outlet room for point-of-sale material?
- Is this the best way to spend your money?
- What is the purpose of the point-of-sale material?
- How long do you expect the material to be used?
- What message do you wish to convey, especially in terms of the product's quality?
- Does your concept tie in with the related media advertising ?
- Is the design of the material identifiably linked with your brand?
- How can you make the point-of-sale material add to the convenience of shoppers?

Store and home demonstrations

Many products, either fast-turnover consumer goods or durable goods, lend themselves to in-store demonstrations. Even better results can be obtained in the home by demonstrating not just to a particular potential customer but at the same time to his or her friends and neighbours.

National and local events

Many national events can be used to help a particular promotion. For example, a promotion of golf bags might be linked to the Open Championship. Local events, such as a shopping-centre opening or a beauty competition, likewise offer a promotional opportunity.

Special magazines

Journals produced by the company can be a useful tool in cases where it is important to build up a continuing loyalty. To be successful, such magazines must be interesting and have some information which the recipient regards as valuable.

Consumer and trade competitions

These are often designed to effect the purchase of the product before entry ('send three wrappers with your form'), and can thus provide a very direct influence on immediate sales. They are valuable also in terms of achieving display and wider distribution of the product. You must pay heed to the laws regarding gambling and lotteries. The competition rules must be carefully screened by the legal department before the competition is announced.

Advantages of sales promotion

These are the major techniques which your company can use to help push the product towards the customer. To conclude this section, let us look at some of the advantages common to all of them.

Product concentration

Promoting one product in the range will sell others of the company's products as well.

Area concentration

Smaller companies can use sales promotions in selected geographical areas to advantage, since major national competitors are likely to be unable to counter specific campaigns at such a local level.

Area response

The effect of a sales promotion is usually much easier to assess than that of an advertising campaign. The levels of selling-in, consumer purchase and re-stocking can be measured to ensure that the sales-promotion technique is being used to optimum effect.

Flexibility

Because results can be measured so quickly, the company is given the opportunity to adapt swiftly from one approach to another and also to take advantage of special local, seasonal or competitive conditions.

Improved advertising

Sales promotion can be used to add strength to an advertising campaign by giving the consumer some tangible advantage and thereby 'topping up' an otherwise general advertising claim.

9 PUBLIC RELATIONS

Simply put, whether a company is selling products or services, its image is at the heart of its marketing effort and is thus a vital part of its success. Other things being equal, a customer's or client's image of a company can make the difference between sale or no sale, success and failure.

A company image is not something a company *has*; rather, it is a composite of the attitudes or impressions the market has about the company. It is based on the combined experience of all those individuals who have used, still use, have stopped using or who have never used its services or products.

Literally everything the company is, says or does affects its image. The company's advertising is the most apparent way in which it communicates the image it would like to have, but popular impressions are based also on countless other factors—printed material, stationery, political stance, packaging or merely the physical appearances of its offices and plant.

Projecting a company image

When the company is planning its public relations it has to distinguish between its *current* image (the image held by people outside the company) and its *mirror* image (the employees' idea of outsiders' impressions). The difference between these images and the company's *optimum* image are the basis of any overall PR. The company has to recognise that effective PR requires a programme that is planned and then reviewed on a regular basis. This does not mean that PR cannot be opportunist—indeed, it must take every opportunity to interact with the company's markets, or 'publics', to use PR terminology. One of the better definitions of PR was given by the Institute of Public Relations, 1987, as can be seen, it reinforces the planning function:

> Public relations practice is the planned and sustained effort to establish and maintain the goodwill and mutual understanding between an organisation and its publics.

The key phrase in this definition is 'planned and sustained'. PR is more than a haphazard, knee-jerk reaction to events: it requires objectives to be in place and a programme that has evolved directly from those objectives.

Advertising is a means of conveying a marketing message which the company controls—not only the message but the timing, reach and frequency of its appearance can be dictated. Press relations, a vital function of PR, by contrast lives or dies at the whim of an editor who probably is not under the company's control. But there is a major advantage to press coverage: it is *clearly not advertising*. It reaches the reader, listener or viewer not as a message from seller to buyer but as something said about the company or its products by a disinterested third party. PR messages are seen by consumers as a more credible source of information than advertising because they are not customarily perceived as *sponsored* messages. For example, a favourable review of a new rock album is likely to sell more copies than an advertisement in the same journal—and costs nothing more than giving the reviewer a free copy of the album. Many people have stopped believing the hyperbole of advertising, but they will believe what the reviewer has to say.

As we noted earlier, advertising has been described as 'mass selling'; it concentrates on a broad theme and attempts to reach as many potential customers as possible for the minimum amount of money. PR, by contrast, can be used to reach small but important market segments and can do so with great cost-effectiveness. As well as supporting the company's major marketing message and gaining the attention of important markets, PR is a very inexpensive way of filling gaps in the total marketing plan. Let's look at a couple of examples. If you advertise during only 20 weeks of the year, PR can keep your company or product in the public eye for the other 32 weeks. If your product is seasonal, PR can be targeted according to your best seasons. Likewise it can be used to reach specific geographical territories or small, select target markets.

PR is far from purely a marketing matter. It can help in social and industrial relations and in dealing with legislative forces that might inhibit the customers' willingness to buy. In marketing terms, such dealings can colour customer attitudes towards the company and its products or erect barriers against your selling messages.

In the field of social relations, PR should do more than create mutual goodwill between the company (and hence its products) and its customers. Good industrial relations can help sales; company employees, if properly motivated, have a close identification with the company and a sense of pride in their contribution to its products. Not only will they buy the products themselves, they will act as word-of-mouth advertisers. Good government relations can help the company avoid doing things that might draw criticism and, no matter how unjustifiably, reflect on the company's integrity.

The company's best PR efforts can be nullified at the point of purchase if a distributor feels that the company has not provided effective service or helped the distributor's business. The matter of distributor relations is essentially concerned with improving distributors' understanding of the company's organisation and those elements of the marketing operation in which company and distributor regularly interact. By improving its own understanding of its distributors' trade attitudes, opinions and problems, the company can help them become more profitable. If the communications link is improved, distributors become better educated about products.

Planning for public relations

The overriding key to getting the best out of PR is to ensure that you have an advance programme, in writing, that includes communications objectives, budgets and a schedule of operational activities (or options). This programme provides what is in essence a checklist of activities which the PR manager or PR consultant can use to chart progress; similarly, the company can use it to measure performance. Deliberate and sustained planning allows you to blend your marketing effort with your PR efforts. Since PR is arguably the most cost-effective tool within the marketing 'mix', this is obviously desirable.

Initially, PR planning is concerned with establishing objectives, identifying target publics, and setting PR (or communications) objectives.

Target publics should be quantified in terms of who, where and how many; also, their attitudes towards the company need to be qualified. A typical (but no means complete) set of target publics might include:

- customers
- prospective customers
- distributors
- specifiers
- intermediaries
- trade training establishments
- professional training establishments
- environmental groups
- special-interest groups

- industry associations
- local and central government
- the company's own staff and prospective staff
- financial advisors
- suppliers

PR objectives are identified in section 6 of the sample briefing given below. It will be seen that they centre on awareness, perception and acceptability levels.

Briefing the PR advisor

The following brief for someone dealing with a PR consultant or advisor is designed to give a comprehensive background analysis in PR terms of, first, where the company is now, and, second, where it wants to go. As with any brief, it will not be used in its entirety at each briefing; rather, it gives a framework whereby full coverage of all the information and of the company marketing aspirations can be ensured.

1 Company background

- provide a company organisation plan, giving the names of all the people with whom the advisor will be dealing
- state who is authorised to approve what
- give details of any market-research facilities, advertising agencies, sales-promotion teams, marketing consultants, and so on, employed by the company

2 The product (or service) profile

- give a brief physical description of the product
- define the product's main intended usage
- describe (concisely) the product's benefits

- state the product's advantages over its competitors
- itemise prices and margins
- advise of special terms, discounts, hire-purchase terms, leasing rights, government legislation, etc.
- suggest the atmosphere and effect required for the PR campaign or activity

3 The competition

- list the product's direct competitors
- identify and comment on competitor products, stressing their strengths as well as their weaknesses
- identify possible future competitors

4 Company and product position relative to competitors

- outline the position relative to the competition in terms of
  market-share trends
  PR activities
  PR expenditure
  pricing and margins
  sales organisations
- summarise
  the image and positioning of the product in the market
  the image and positioning of the product in respect to the consumer's or end-user's perceptions

5 Product sales and PR history

- outline the PR support given to the product over the previous twelve months, detailing publicity and press-relations methods used and the results obtained
- outline the advertising/sales-promotion support given to the product over the same period
- outline the sales history of the product

- outline the PR, advertising and sales-promotion histories of the competitor products—themes, media used, expenditure, and so on
- outline the sales histories of the competitor products

6 PR objectives

- itemise, as applicable, your PR objectives in terms of the following:
  user-awareness level
  consumer-awareness level
  user-perception level
  consumer-perception level
  user-acceptability level
  consumer-acceptability level
  promotional objectives:
    to get the product tried
    to increase purchase frequency
    to encourage product (or brand) switch
    to generate goodwill
    to support distributors
    to impress distributors
    to convey technical data
    to improve the morale of the sales force
- depending on how confidential its contents are, supply as much as possible of the product marketing plan containing the PR/marketing objectives
- ask the advisor to confirm that the proposed campaign can relate to the achievement of these objectives

7 The market/publics

- identify target markets (publics)
  who uses the product?
  who buys the product?
  who decides on the choice of product?

- quantify size of market (public)
  - number of potential customers at consumer level
  - number of potential customers at distributor level
  - geographical distribution of the market (public)
- comment on habits, attitudes and usage
  - how is the product used?
  - where is the product used?
  - why is the product used?
  - when is the product used?
  - buyer likes and dislikes
- comment on whether customers' decisions to buy the product are generally
  - on impulse
  - through habit
  - after careful consideration
- make available all pertinent information from research sources relating to
  - market information in terms of size and structure
  - market information in terms of attitudes, habits, likes and dislikes
  - product testing and product information
  - the media

8 Sales and distribution

- detail all the distribution methods used for the product
- outline all distributor-relations activities, both current and past
- give information about the size, organisational structure and selling responsibilities of the sales force
- spell out details of the sales aids the sales force requires
- summarise longer-term aims concerning relations with the distribution channels

9 Advisor commitments and timetable

- state company requirements regarding use of
  - design studios
  - graphic artists
  - printers
  - packaging consultants
  - video producers/companies
  - audio producers/companies
  - other suppliers
- state the company's requirements concerning the presentation of its 'corporate identity' in terms of
  - typefaces
  - colour schemes
  - other restrictions
- say how the PR campaign's performance standards will be judged in terms of
  - the stated objectives (see section 6 on PR objectives)
  - other measurable benchmarks
- suggest start and finish dates for the PR activity, as well as the geographical area that should be covered
- request specific publicity and press-relations activities
- state required dates for
  - creative recommendations
  - PR-plan recommendations
- say what is the required lead time for approval of any of the above recommendations
- detail the company's sales cycles and/or promotional plans
- set out the proposed PR, advertising and product-launch date(s)
- give special instructions for promotional material in as much detail and as clearly as possible

Public and press relations procedures

Once target publics have been identified and measurable communications objectives determined, PR activity takes the form of a carefully constructed, continuous programme. The company can use numerous PR techniques and procedures. Among these are:

- annual reports
- surveys of customer opinion
- corporate-identity programmes:
  internal (stationery, decor, employees' uniforms, etc.)
  external (signage, packaging, etc.)
- corporate (or institutional) advertising
- press releases (personal, product, facilities, technical information, etc.)
- feature articles
- technical publications
- customer newsletters
- educational reference material
- exhibitions
- trade displays
- documentaries (audio, video, audiovisual, etc.)
- press conferences
- personal appearances
- special events
- company literature
- open-house sessions
- sponsorships
- awards
- case studies
- testimonials
- employee relations
- recruitment advertising

- personnel induction
- training and self-development
- procedure manuals
- suggestion schemes
- performance standards
- house newsletters
- house journals
- incentives

To ensure the above techniques are used to maximum effect and to make the best use of the company's PR counsel within the programme you should

- call in the PR advisor whenever you require to communicate with your target publics, whether this is a planned activity or an 'unexpected' marketing opportunity
- see that the advisor is involved in all meetings affecting the company's marketing policy
- hold regular planning or coordinating meetings to evaluate all PR activities
- set up procedures relating to the approval of all printed copy or other PR materials
- establish how the attainment of the objectives will be measured
- keep the advisor up-to-date on all company operations

Make your PR advisors full members of the company's marketing team by keeping them informed about objectives, budgets, advertising or promotional goals and activities, market-research findings, and changes of plan. There is no way you can *over-inform* your PR advisors—but there are countless ways in which you can hamper the PR programme through *under-informing* them.

CONSUMER BEHAVIOUR

Human wants are numerous, complex, imperfectly understood and constantly changing. Marketing managers have to do their best to analyse the human wants and desires relevant to their company and its products. This process is known as market determination or segmentation. If a product's market has more than two buyers it is capable of being segmented—i.e., meaningfully divided into distinct groups of buyers.

Segmenting a market requires the answers to a series of specific questions. Is there a market? How big is the market? Where is it? What are its characteristics?

Once the product is submitted for market consideration, judgment is in the hands of the consumer. Generally consumers seek wider selection, better quality, more advantages, less trouble, greater economy and a feeling of accomplishment in the purchase and use of the product(s).

However, before we look more closely at the motives and habits of buyers, let us glance at the factors that together comprise the market's overall structure.

Market structure

Numerous factors affect the structure of a market—among them are general population, the make-up of families, income levels, the sex of potential buyers, marital status, age, occupation, mobility, education, proportion of wage earners, city or town size, geographical differences of preference, conformity and individuality.

For many products the family is a more important unit than the individual. Cars, domestic appliances, furniture and many other major and minor items are typically bought by families.

The family's income, while it does not entirely determine purchasing patterns, is one of the basic influences on buying. Discretionary spending is evident in today's market, as is an increasing tendency to reduce purchasing in order to save for later purchasing or for other purposes.

There are more women working than ever before, and many of them are married; of these, a high proportion work not to support a family but to provide funds for 'extras'. According to various surveys, women's influence on family purchasing of durable products runs from 35 per cent (e.g. cameras) to 85 per cent (e.g. furniture). When it comes to food the percentages can be even higher. This dominance of the consumer market by women and the level of the promotions resulting from it are accented by increasing ease of purchase, knowledge of choices, and the appeal of 'bargain' shopping.

Each age-group needs certain products that are irrelevant to people who are older or younger. Pop records provide a classic example: teenagers usually have hardly even heard of the artistes whose records their parents buy, and *vice versa*. It is worth noting that the sections of the market aged under 20 and over 85 are both expanding.

A number of consumer attitudes have a basic effect on consumption patterns. These include whether or not:

- there is general approval of, and use of, credit
- the virtue of spending is extolled
- the constant appearance of new products is accepted as normal
- there is more leisure time .

- fashion influences buying
- the average worker is more valued and better paid
- there is general confidence in the future

At the moment, a large part of the market derives from the fact that people are trading up: more and more of them buy products because they perceive them to be better than the ones they already have. Fashion is becoming more important in many fields. Simultaneously, services are becoming more important to the consumer.

Why people buy

All behaviour is motivated, and the selection of which product a consumer buys is no exception. How to influence customers to buy is no simple matter: each and every purchase is the result of a complex interaction of motives and gratuitous influences. People are usually ignorant of most of the influences which affect them; of the few that they recognise, perhaps a couple of per cent can be accurately and usefully described to someone else.

Motives work in cycles. These start whenever a person feels a need: he or she is stirred into increasing amounts of activity until the need is satisfied, at which point the current cycle ends. As satisfaction wears off the need grows again, so that a new motivational cycle starts. The actions that secured satisfaction last time are likely to be repeated, to the detriment of those which were ineffectual before. Thus the behaviour pattern associated with satisfying needs becomes streamlined and habitual (a process called instrumental learning). At the simplest level, consumers will stick with the companies whose products have satisfied their needs in the past, while avoiding like the plague any brand whose product has let them down.

Throughout the individual's lifespan motives cyclically

appear, develop and decay. This cycle is a product of instrumental learning, environmental changes, physical and psychological maturation, and the interesting process whereby primary motives generate secondary needs (as in the way that the need for food generates a need for money). Occasionally, secondary motives become primary—for example, the needs for money, power, speed and cigarettes.

Motivational cycles frequently meet blocks (as when products or brands become unobtainable). This creates frustration which can be relieved only when substitutes are found; substitutes are likely to become permanent replacements. Again, motives often conflict: should I buy something that is not exactly what I want, or should I simply save the money for something else? A different form of internal conflict takes place in the consumer faced by alternative brands that promise equal satisfaction.

Motivation research

Information about motivation is harder to get from the consumer or potential consumer than information about how they buy. The term 'motivation research' encompasses the series of methods and techniques designed to discover why people (particularly ultimate consumers) act or think as they do. It uses the techniques of insight application, attribute association, projective tests and depth interviewing to obtain 'reason-why' information. There are several methods, including:

- individual in-depth interview
- group discussions
- word-association testing
- sentence-completion testing
- picture-association tests
- personality-situation tests

The disadvantages of motivation research are frequently cited: they include lack of reliability (because the sample of people tested is small), expense, and the difficulty of translating any findings into marketing terms. However, the marketing manager who understands motivation can more effectively tune in to the consumers' buying responses, however incomplete and unsatisfactory his or her understanding might be.

General consumer behaviour

There are several identifiable motivations and influences, some personal and some social. Primary social influences are the opinions of one's peer group. Individual motivations are classified as rational, emotional or concerned with patronage:

- *rational motives* are concerned with profit/gain, economy of purchase/use, product versatility, product re-sale value, convenience, dependability, durability and protection value
- *emotional motives* can be categorised as the search for advantage, dominance, security, wealth, position, social recognition, prestige, emulation, satisfaction of the senses, pleasure/happiness, diversion/recreation, comfort or physical well-being, individuality, conformity, creativeness . . .
- *patronage motives* relate to why people choose one outlet rather than another—price preference, location, convenience, variety of goods available, merchandise quality, services rendered, personal relationships, general reputation, distribution advantages, reciprocal trade considerations, etc.

Motivations can be differentiated in other ways. One system

involves depicting motivational conflicts that occur during each act of purchase:

- individual *vs* family purchasing
- primary (deciding) motives *vs* secondary (auxiliary) motives
- general motives *vs* particular motives
- conscious motives *vs* dormant motives
- psychological (individual) motives *vs* psychogenic (social) motives

These motives vary in their strength and effect between different people as well as within the same person at different times.

Consumer behaviour theories

The ultimate marketing aim of a company is to work out its market. This entails knowing who the customers are, what they want, how they buy and how they use and react to a product. The market environment and its effect on the buyer in terms of price, product features, advertising message and corporate image likewise need to be known.

There are four standard theories about consumer behaviour described here, of which the last two are more generally acceptable to marketing management—although it has to be realised that the actions of individual consumers rarely match permanently with any of these theories.

The traditional theory is the Marshallian Economic Model, now generally discredited. The theory claims that economic factors alone explain variations in sales. It sees consumers behaving in an entirely rational manner, carefully calculating the effect of the consequences of his or her purchases, carefully assessing such factors as price and value, and making an optimum choice. The model completely ignores a fundamental question: how are product and brand preferences formed?

The Freudian Model is based on psychoanalytical ideas of motivation. Since Freud's time many refinements and changes in emphasis have been made. The marketing implication of this model is that buyers are motivated not just by economic-functional product concerns but also by symbols. Motivation research based on this model can and often does lead to useful insights into buyer behaviour, but it can also lead to deceptive and misleading findings.

The Pavlovian Learning Model views consumers' buying behaviour as an associative process. The theory has four central concepts: drive (the consumer's individual stimulus impelling him or her into taking action), cues (the stimuli from the environment), response (the buyer's reaction to the cues), and reinforcement (the tendency to repeat rewarding experiences so that responses recur). The strategy of advertising and copy-writing is often developed according to the Pavlovian theory.

The Veblenian Social-Psychological Model has as its basis the view that the attitudes and behaviour of human beings are influenced by several levels of society—culture, subculture, social class, group and family. The individual's wants and behaviour are largely moulded by his/her present 'group' membership and the group to which he/she aspires. This model has been much used in marketing as a way of segmenting markets. Small groups with whom the buyer comes into contact can have a powerful effect on his/her attitudes. Social influences determine many, but not all, of the behavioural variations people display: two individuals subjected to the same influences will quite probably have different attitudes. And neither do attitudes automatically guarantee certain types of behaviour. The buying process is in itself a learning experience, and can bring about a change in attitudes. According to this theory the buying process has five stages:

- a need
- pre-purchase activity
- the purchase decision
- product use
- post-purchase feelings

According to this theory, then, the marketer must introduce into his or her series of messages such factors as specificness, authority, impact and credibility.

Industrial buying habits

There is a fifth theory concerning the way in which buyers behave—the Hobbesian Organisation Model. This is the only buyer-behaviour theory to have been developed concerning industrial purchases. The model holds that the industrial buyer balances his or her own personal needs with those of the organisation. The implications are that organisational buyers can be appealed to on both personal and organisational grounds. The best 'mix' varies from buyer to buyer and from product to product, as well as depending upon the nature of the organisation. Where the products offered are much the same in terms of quality and price, the buyer can be swayed more easily by personal or emotive factors. If there are great differences in the products, the buyer pays more attention to rational factors.

The marketing of industrial products has a number of characteristics that distinguish it from consumer marketing:

- the geographic clustering of its markets
- the economic concentration of industrial expenditure: in the UK, 20 per cent of companies account for 80 per cent of all industrial purchases
- direct distribution from producer to user is the norm
- product demands do not depend directly upon consumer increase or decrease in income

- unlike consumer products, where product decision is made by an individual or family group, industrial products are typically bought by disparate people
- the pattern of industrial purchasing is more irregular than that of consumer purchasing—buying is a product of necessity (rather than of the wish to satisfy a desire), and depends upon the movement of goods that consume industrial materials
- industrial products are rented and leased to a greater extent than are consumer goods
- reciprocity is still a factor in industrial purchasing
- industrial purchasers often buy in large units, and such sales are often preceded by long periods of negotiation
- multiple purchasing so as to obtain an optimum or advantageous quantity
- the industrial buyer is *knowledgeable* about his or her purchase
- the buying atmosphere is formal and informative rather than informal and dependent upon superficial appeal
- emotion has importance only insofar as the buyer is trying to do a satisfactory job for his or her company
- industrial products are bought only after inspection, sampling or careful consideration of the descriptions supplied by the manufacturer

SETTING MARKETING OBJECTIVES

In many companies, management by the setting of marketing objectives contributes significantly to improved management and results. We can define this as a systematic approach which sets out to link the company goals of profit and growth to individual managers' needs to contribute and develop themselves to the full. The use of objectives is particularly effective in marketing because the relationship between cause and effect is not always as clear in marketing as it is in other company functions and so effort can, with the best of intentions, easily be misdirected.

In this chapter we shall discuss briefly the introduction and operation of an objectives-based approach. We should note at the outset that, while the performance of *company* objectives is not a matter that immediately concerns us, the determination of them at company or corporate level is far from easy: it requires plenty of time and mental effort. Indefinite and vague objectives are, as you might expect, unsatisfactory. Corporate objectives are usually set over the functions of marketing, production, technical, distribution, administration, manpower and finance. The essence of the objective-setting approach to marketing is the *total* review and integration of the company's marketing goals with those of individual managers.

Integration of marketing objectives and corporate medium-range plans

Unless medium-range plans have been prepared, the marketing objectives will remain little more than pious hopes. The medium-range plan must outline the policies and strategies to be employed by the company in order to reach its marketing objectives.

Determination of marketing objectives

In most companies of any size, the corporate objectives are insufficiently detailed to serve as a practical guide to the required actions of a single function. Consequently, the relevant corporate objectives must be broken down into detail to derive the objectives for each individual function.

When determining marketing objectives, it is vital to ensure that they are realistic, can be achieved by the unit and are compatible with the conditions and strategies set out in the company's medium-range plan. They must also contribute to and concord with corporate objectives. Finally, before they are signed and sealed, they should be agreed by the marketing manager.

The first step is to examine and clarify the role of the marketing unit *as a whole* in the company's corporate plan. For example, while sales objectives may be clear, analysis might reveal that other aspects of the unit's required contribution to the overall objectives have not been sufficiently thought out.

The process of relating the objectives of the marketing unit to the short- and long-term goals of the corporate plan is participative, in that it takes heed of the ideas and suggestions of the heads of all the marketing functions concerned. If reviews are regularly conducted between individual managers and top management, the corporate plan will embody the best ideas from each level.

Identifying key areas

The term 'key areas' describes marketing-management activities that have to be coordinated to achieve the really important results. In terms of the total number of tasks the unit has to perform, such activities may amount to only 20 per cent, but their influence on the successful performance of the job can easily be as much as 80 per cent.

Regular re-examination and review of activities in the key areas can reveal that effort is being misdirected. As in other fields of the objectives-setting approach, the analysis of results in the key areas is most effective when it is genuinely participative, drawing on the contributions and commitment of managers at every level.

Agreeing the performance expectations of each manager

The best results are achieved by managers who are clear about what is expected of them in each important part of their job, and who are personally committed to achieving this. All managers share five basic needs:

- agree with me what is expected of me
- give me the opportunity to achieve the agreed results
- let me know how I am getting on
- help, guide and train me
- reward me according to my contribution

Analysing key areas is probably the most difficult step in marketing objective-setting, but it is also one of the most rewarding. In effect, it involves analysing the job of the unit head, in terms of the corporate and unit objectives, and isolating the key areas where effort should be directed.

The first analysis usually identifies a mixture of key tasks, individual jobs, less essential tasks, and incomplete, vague or inappropriate tasks. In a number of key result areas the activities of an individual marketing manager may significantly influence the overall effort. These areas are usually among the following:

- profitability
- market share
- product development
- market intelligence
- costs
- consumer satisfaction
- sales management
- finance
- manufacturing or production relations
- product quality
- promotional activity

From the key-results analysis of each manager's job, the following should emerge:

- the manager's key tasks
- the manager's priority plan
- suggestions for action requiring authority beyond that of the individual manager—items which could possibly appear on the company's short-range action plans

The understanding and commitment of each key marketing manager are brought about by regular discussion with top management. The aim of these discussions is agreement on the manager's required standards of performance.

Marketing management control methods

For each of the key tasks a standard of performance must be agreed between the marketing manager and his or her superior. This standard represents the best level of performance that the manager agrees can realistically be achieved. In other words, a high but attainable standard.

After agreement has been reached as to what constitutes a satisfactory standard, it is necessary to examine how performance of the key tasks is controlled. This may show that the control of vital aspects of the job performance is inadequate. Such examinations can be fruitful even in apparently straightforward job areas such as the management of sales representatives. For example, the sales force of one company was selling to chemists. Analysis revealed that the sales manager had totally inadequate control over the vital task of training salesmen. The result of this discovery was that new methods were introduced to monitor the extent and effectiveness of each branch manager's on-the-job training activities.

Attention should be given not just to the adequacy of the control information which superiors receive concerning their subordinates' performances. The person who can take the best and most immediate corrective action is the job performer him- or herself, and so it is worth making sure that the right control information is being given directly to that individual.

Creating marketing action plans

The participatory aspect of the objective-setting approach goes a long way towards revealing the real problems and obstacles that prevent individuals from contributing their best. Sometimes the system itself is improved through better understanding of which aspects are the current priorities and which are now less important, clearer agreement between manager and subordinates on precisely what constitutes satisfactory results in a key area, or recognition of the need for better methods of control.

Sometimes the action required is organisational. Some plans may be for the individuals, others for a team. All define who must do what and by when the required change is to be brought about.

Action plans take various forms, but a simple list of actions to be taken, arranged in order of priority, can be as effective as something more elaborate.

Marketing planning review procedures

An essential part of the total marketing concept is the carrying out of *regular review and assessment*. At least every three months, the job holder and top management should discuss and review the state of progress towards the agreed objectives. These review sessions allow the manager to:

- assess the subordinate's performance
- suggest how to deal with problems
- understand the subordinate's problems
- train the subordinate
- assess the subordinate's potential
- plan future action to help the subordinate to achieve objectives
- listen to suggestions for improvement
- let the subordinate know how he or she is getting on with the job (although this will to a large extent be obvious to

the subordinate from comparison of the achieved level of performance with the agreed target level)

These review sessions also allow the subordinate to:

- report success in meeting objectives
- explain difficulties and problems that have been met
- elicit the aid of a superior in overcoming difficulties
- plan future action to enable objectives to be met
- learn how to deal with problems
- state where there are weaknesses, or where he or she may not have been given the means to achieve the agreed objectives
- put forward suggestions for improvement

To repeat, setting marketing objectives needs time, careful preparation and thought. Either an individual or a small team working within the company must be given the time and have the expertise to guide managers through the process of analysis, job definition and job review. The success of installing clearly defined and measurable marketing objectives as a *continuing* and effective marketing tool depends on the following factors:

- Top marketing management must take the lead in introducing the objectives, and must be visibly convinced of their potential benefits. These managers must be directly involved in setting overall objectives and in the subsequent planning and monitoring of action.
- Everyone involved in the setting of marketing objectives must be in no doubt as to its purpose. Careful preliminary briefing is essential. All managers must understand that the primary purpose of a job review is to produce a plan of action, not a report of past performance. Re-examination of the major purposes and priorities of the job is not an easy task for any manager or group of managers – most

people are resistant to change – but everyone must fully accept that it is necessary.

- If creative action is to be stimulated there must be frequent inputs of interest and guidance from senior management. Performance reviews must not be too infrequent.

INDEX